Judy B. Gilbert

W9-AAU-590

CLEAR SPEECH

FROM THE START

Basic Pronunciation and Listening Comprehension in North American English

Teacher's Resource Book

CAMBRIDGE
UNIVERSITY PRESS

PUBLISHED BY THE PRESS SYNDICATE OF THE UNIVERSITY OF CAMBRIDGE
The Pitt Building, Trumpington Street, Cambridge, United Kingdom

CAMBRIDGE UNIVERSITY PRESS
The Edinburgh Building, Cambridge CB2 2RU, UK
40 West 20th Street, New York, NY 10011–4211, USA
477 Williamstown Road, Port Melbourne, VIC 3207, Australia
Ruiz de Alarcón 13, 28014 Madrid, Spain
Dock House, The Waterfront, Cape Town 8001, South Africa

http://www.cambridge.org

First published 2001
2nd printing 2001

Printed in the United States of America

Typeface Sabon   *System* Quark XPress® [AH]

ISBN 0 521 63737 6   Student's Book   ISBN 0 521 63736 8   Audio Cassettes
ISBN 0 521 63735 X   Teacher's Resource Book   ISBN 0 521 79966 X   Audio CDs

Book design, art direction, and layout services: Adventure House, NYC

Contents

Phonetic Symbol Key

The lists below show how the symbols of the *International Phonetic Alphabet* are used in this book to indicate pronunciation. Next to each symbol are one or two English words in which the sound represented by the symbol occurs. This Phonetic Symbol Key is based on the pronunciation system used in the *Cambridge Dictionary of American English*.

Vowel Symbols

æ	bat, hand
ɑ	hat, barn
ɑɪ	bite, sky
ɑʊ	house, now
e	bet, head
eɪ	late, play
ɪ	fit, bid
iː	feet, please
ɔː	saw, dog
ɔɪ	boy, join
oʊ	go, boat
ʊ	put, good
uː	rude, boot
ʌ	cut, love
ɜ	bird, fur *(used only before /r/ in stressed syllables)*
ə	sitter, alone

Other Symbols

ˈ	*Stress mark placed before a syllable with the heaviest stress, as before the first syllable of* **lemon** /ˈlem•ən/
ˌ	*Stress mark placed before a syllable with lighter stress, as before the second syllable of* **cucumber** /ˈkjuːˌkʌm•bər/
•	*The raised dot separates syllables.*

Consonant Symbols

b	bid, job
d	do, lady
dʒ	jump, bridge
f	foot, safe
g	go, dog
h	home, behind
j	yes, onion
k	kiss, come
l	look, pool
m	many, some
n	need, open
ŋ	sing, sink
p	pen, hope
r	road, card
s	see, recent
ʃ	shoe, nation
t	team, meet
t̪	meeting, latter
θ	think, both
ð	this, father
tʃ	choose, rich
v	visit, save
w	watch, away
z	zoo, these

Acknowledgments

Many teachers contributed ideas for techniques, but I especially want to thank the following:

William Acton, Nagoya, Japan, for his concepts of "Walkabout," page T-23, "Syllablettes," page T-45, and many other ideas for using physical action, pages T-13 and T-54.

Also using a similar concept of walking while talking are Anne Isaac of Melbourne, Australia, and Martha Szabados of Budapest, Hungary.

Elcio C. Alves de Souza, Sao Paulo, Brazil, for the spelling game, page T-11.

Olle Kjellin, M.D., Brantasa, Sweden, for the Choral Approach, with multiple repetition, pages T-6 and T-43–T-44.

Sandra Marttinen, Sacramento, California, for the walking map, page T-88.

Amalia Sarabasa, Caracas, Venezuela, for the term "saturation" teaching.

Jennifer Bixby, Nada Gordon, and Jane Mairs for many good teaching tips and vigilant editing.

Letter to the Teacher

For years, teachers have been asking me to write a version of my intermediate-level book, *Clear Speech*, that would be usable for beginners. They said that it would make more sense to help students with pronunciation early, rather than wait until they have developed habits that are hard to overcome. Also, teachers often found that their beginning students became discouraged when people didn't understand what they were saying, and of course, a discouraged student is harder to teach. Teachers who were trying to help their beginning students with pronunciation expressed frustration with the limited results they were getting from traditional methods of drilling minimal pairs (e.g., *ship/sheep*) or asking students to "sound out" the letters in print. They were asking for a more effective approach.

All of this made sense to me. But the problem was that I just couldn't think of an approach that would work. For one thing, beginners simply don't have enough vocabulary to understand explanations. And with so much else to learn, there isn't much class time for pronunciation. One thing was clear to me: A really useful book had to be radically different from any other in the field, including my own intermediate-level book.

Over time, through much research and discussion, I developed a list of the essential elements of a pronunciation book for beginning students. These six essential elements are listed below. This list describes my approach to teaching beginning pronunciation and the approach taken in this text.

1 Concepts are taught through visual images instead of through words.

Students with little vocabulary have trouble processing written or spoken explanation. Therefore, I have used visuals as much as possible. For example:

- Extra-wide letters are used to show that strong (stressed) vowels last longer.

  ban a na

- Diminishing letters are used to show how a continuant sound continues.

  busss   bellll

- *Music of English* boxes teach melody and rhythm in common phrases using pitch lines and extra-wide letters.

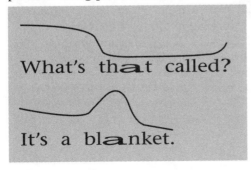

- Drawings and even photographs are used to show the tongue position for different sounds. In addition to showing views of the mouth from the side and from the top, a new perspective has been added: looking toward the front of the mouth, the way most people actually visualize their tongues.

2 Only the most crucial sounds are presented, leaving the rest for later study.

Because beginning students have so much else to learn, it is practical to focus their attention only on the most important sounds. These are the sounds that act as grammar cues, such as the plural *s* and the past tense *d*.

3 Every teaching point is designed not only to help intelligibility but also to improve listening comprehension.

The most fundamental aspects of English pronunciation are also essential to listening comprehension. Therefore, to maximize the benefit to students, all new topics are first introduced through listening tasks in which students learn to hear the crucial distinctions before they begin to produce them.

4 Rhythm is taught through the visual and kinesthetic modes.

Most language learners unconsciously transfer the rhythm of their first language to any new language, which can seriously hamper their ability to communicate. Because rhythm is so instinctual and so physical, this book teaches the rhythm of English through visual and kinesthetic activities. Students tap out syllables and use rubber bands to practice lengthening stressed syllables, and the *Music of English* boxes use extra-wide letters to draw students' attention to the rhythm patterns of English speech.

5 Immediate help with reading is provided by teaching simple spelling rules.

Beginning students need to learn how to pronounce words based on their spelling so that they can read English with some accuracy. This book presents a few very basic rules for decoding combinations of letters (spelling) so that students can figure out how a particular spelling might be pronounced.

6 Tasks emphasize phrases, not just individual words.

People learn pronunciation best in whole fixed phrases, like the lyrics of a song. Learning the whole phrase rather than individual words imprints the rhythm, melody, and linking of the phrase. Short "musical" phrases are graphically presented in the *Music of English* boxes, providing students with useful language.

The only way to assure that a book truly works in the classroom is to have many cycles of field testing by teachers working in different countries, at different levels, with different kinds of students. Many teachers around the world participated in this process. I hope their efforts will make the book a pleasure for you to use.

Judy B. Gilbert

Introduction

Teacher's Resource Book Features

This Teacher's Resource Book includes the following features to help teachers manage the course more effectively:

Unit Overviews   Each unit begins with an outline of its main teaching points, to facilitate class planning.

Reduced Student's Book Pages with Answers   Each page of the Teacher's Resource Book contains a reduced version of the Student's Book page it relates to. These reduced pages are identical to the pages in the Student's Book, except that the answers have been filled in.

Task Descriptions with Notes on Presentation   The task descriptions are accompanied by a variety of presentation ideas as well as useful theoretical background information.

Audio Script with Phonetic Transcriptions   An audio script is provided for all of the material on the audio program that does not appear on the pages of the Student's Book. This audio script includes phonetic transcriptions. Teachers can use the transcriptions as a pronunciation guideline when reading the sections themselves, or to help clarify pronunciation of specific items for students.

Teaching Tips   Throughout the book there are teaching tips marked by a lightbulb icon. These are expansion activities that reinforce or extend the points students are learning in the unit. These activities can add more fun and variety to lessons.

Photocopiable Quizzes   Units 1–15 come with photocopiable, 10-point quizzes for teachers' convenience. They are designed to be given after the completion of each unit. Answers to the quizzes and the quiz audio script are given in the Quiz Answer Key.

Audio CD with Recorded Quizzes   The audio CD that comes with this Teacher's Resource Book contains the audio portion of the photocopiable quizzes for Units 1–15.

Course Overview

This course is designed to give beginning students immediate help with English pronunciation. It concentrates on teaching those elements of pronunciation that will make the biggest difference in students' ability to understand the speech of others and to make themselves understood. The course is also intended to help students make use of English spelling by learning how to spell words, how to ask about spelling, and how to decode common spelling patterns.

Because beginners have so much to learn, this course presents only those aspects of pronunciation that are most urgently needed, leaving other issues for later study. Important skills and concepts are presented through graphic images, whenever possible, and recycled throughout the course in topic strands. These topic strands include the following:

- **The alphabet:** Using English letters to spell aloud in order to repair misunderstandings quickly.

- **Decoding spelling:** Using simple and efficient spelling rules to guess how a word is pronounced. Armed with these rules, students can use their books to practice what they learn in class.

- **Important sound contrasts:** Focusing on the presence or absence of the sounds that matter the most. These are the sounds that carry important grammatical meaning, such as the final -*d* that marks the past tense (as in *paid*), the final -*s* that indicates plural (as in *books*), and the final -*s* that marks verbs as third-person singular (as in *talks*).

- **Syllable number:** Developing a greater awareness of syllables, and overcoming the tendency to add or drop syllables and thereby obscure meaning. Learners often leave out small words like *the* or word endings like -*ing* because they do not have a strong sense of the number of syllables in a word or sentence.

- **Strong and weak syllables (stressed and de-stressed):** Lengthening vowels in stressed or strong syllables and shortening vowels in de-stressed or weak syllables. Because stress is so important in English, and is often used to focus attention on key words in a sentence, this kind of rhythm training can make a major difference in intelligibility.

- **Linking:** Linking words together. Students often have difficulty figuring out where a word ends and another one begins because of the English pattern of linking wherever possible. Practice with linking can help their listening comprehension.

- **The Music of English:** Learning the intonation and rhythm of English through communicative practice with sentences that are especially useful for beginners, such as:

    - How do you spell *time*?
    - What does *paid* mean?
    - What's that called? What's it for?
    - How do you pronounce L - E - S - S?
    - Did you say *cold*? No, I said *coal*.
    - Where is it? What is it?

Making the Most of the Student's Book

Using the Artwork Illustrations of many of the key words used in tasks are provided to help students learn the new vocabulary. When important sound contrasts are introduced, starting in Unit 8, illustrations of the mouth positions are provided from different perspectives, including from the inside of the mouth looking to the front. In the *looking to the front* drawings, blue spaces are used to represent the shape of the openings through which air flows out of the mouth. In the *looking down* and *looking to the side* drawings, blue arrows represent this airflow to the outside. For additional help you can use the face diagram in Appendix A of the Student's Book to point out the parts of the mouth used for forming different sounds. You can also use the photographs of the wax models if you prefer.

Throughout the book, words set on a blue background represent spoken English. Unconventional spelling is often used in these spoken forms to illustrate a pronunciation feature, while the written version is shown with conventional spelling in black print on a white background. Pointing this out can help students distinguish between the spelled version and the spoken version.

Pitch lines (especially in the *Music of English* boxes) can help students sense what they need to do musically. Some students find it helpful to actually draw these lines themselves. Others find drawing pitch lines frustrating, so it is best not to require students to do it. Instead, you can illustrate the pitch pattern on the board yourself.

Using Listening Exercises Focused listening activities provide a solid foundation for confident, accurate speaking. Allow enough time for students to be sure of what they are hearing. Whenever the Student's Book instructions ask students to listen again, the listening will be repeated on the audio program. You can, however, tailor the listening exercises to fit the specific needs of your students. For example, more advanced classes may not need a second listening in some cases, and other classes may need to hear certain tasks a third time. If students need more time between task items, press the pause button on your CD or cassette player. It is a good idea to periodically ask for student feedback on the pace of the listening exercises so you can adjust your approach accordingly. If the audio program is not available, you can read listening exercises aloud from the audio scripts in the book.

Music of English These boxes present useful sentences to help students build an internal sense of the music of the language. You can encourage your students by repeating the sentences yourself several times before you have them speak. The more enthusiastically and expressively you repeat the phrases, the more students will feel free to be enthusiastic and expressive as well. Then give your class plenty of choral repetition practice, so that individual students can build confidence by first repeating as a synchronized group. This way they will absorb the rhythm and melody of the key sentences so that they will be able to use them with ease and accuracy.

Sometimes the *Music of English* boxes contain linked exchanges or conversations rather than isolated phrases. In such cases, have your students say the exchange as a whole piece after doing the task, to develop a sense of how the meaning and the intonation patterns are linked.

Pair Work Student pair work is a frequently occurring task that gives students the opportunity to practice what they are learning. It is valuable for students to try each task with different partners. This not only allows more repetition of the practice items for each task, but also affords practice in hearing varied pronunciation. Even if your students all speak the same first language, their English pronunciation will vary. In fact, each time the same person says something, there is likely to be some variation. That is why listening to an actual person speak is more useful than listening to the same recorded item over and over.

The format for pair work tasks can be changed to hold students' attention. The same task can be done in pairs, small groups, the whole class, or the class divided into halves. Repetition can also be done in a whisper, or as exaggerated "singing" of the intonation line.

Using Physical Activities Many physical activities are suggested in the task descriptions to reinforce rhythm and intonation patterns. Physical actions, such as stretching a rubber band or moving your hands apart, can convey the concept of lengthening a vowel, for example. For practice of syllable number, you can have students tap on the desks with their pencils, clap their hands, or stamp their feet. Other kinesthetic actions such as hand gestures, raising eyebrows, rising from the seat a little, or even full walking exercises (if space allows), can be very useful in helping students internalize the rhythms and intonations of English.

CLEAR SPEECH
FROM THE START

Teacher's Resource Book

1 The alphabet and vowels

Unit overview

This unit introduces the letters of the alphabet, with special attention paid to the vowels. Students need immediate help figuring out how to pronounce written English, so that they can practice on their own what they have learned in class. English spelling is complicated and, unlike many other languages, the letter combinations are not always pronounced in the same way. The vowel letters are particularly challenging because each one represents at least two different sounds. Also, some of these sounds may not exist in the student's first language.

The traditional approach for teaching English-speaking children how to read by "sounding out the letters" is not really suitable for students who do not know all the sounds of English yet (e.g., the /æ/ in *cat* or the /ɪ/ in *sit*). This course takes a completely different approach, more appropriate to second-language learners.

🎧 A The alphabet

Students will hear the names of each letter in the alphabet. This exercise is just for listening: Ask students not to pronounce the letter names yet. (That will begin in Unit 2.) Encouraging students to hold off on producing new sounds (or words) gives them a chance to develop a clear acoustic imprint of these sounds and avoids confusing them with their own attempts at production before they are ready.

1 The alphabet and vowels

Cake, please.

🎧 A The alphabet

Listen.

Aa Bb Cc Dd Ee Ff Gg Hh Ii Jj Kk Ll Mm Nn
Oo Pp Qq Rr Ss Tt Uu Vv Ww Xx Yy Zz

🎧 B Vowel letters

Listen.

A E I O U

🎧 C Do you hear A?

1 Listen. Mark Yes or No.

	Yes	No	
1.	✓		(cake)
2.		✓	(rice)
3.	✓		
4.		✓	
5.		✓	
6.	✓		

A

cake

2 Listen again.

🎧 D Do you hear E?

1 Listen. Mark Yes or No.

	Yes	No	
1.	✓		(tea)
2.	✓		
3.		✓	
4.	✓		
5.		✓	
6.	✓		

E

tea

2 Listen again.

🎧 C Do you hear A?

Exercises C through G help students learn to identify the vowels, an important step before being asked to say them.

Audio script

1. cake	/keɪk/
2. rice	/raɪs/
3. pay	/peɪ/
4. so	/soʊ/
5. seat	/siːt/
6. make	/meɪk/

🎧 D Do you hear E?

Audio script

1. tea	/tiː/
2. key	/kiː/
3. toe	/toʊ/
4. cheese	/tʃiːz/
5. two	/tuː/
6. please	/pliːz/

See page v for a key to the phonetic symbols.

🎧 **E** *Do you hear I?*

1 Listen. Mark Yes or No.

	Yes	No
1.	✓	
2.	✓	
3.		✓
4.	✓	
5.	✓	
6.		✓

I

ice

2 Listen again.

🎧 **F** *Do you hear O?*

1 Listen. Mark Yes or No.

	Yes	No
1.	✓	
2.	✓	
3.	✓	
4.		✓
5.	✓	
6.		✓

O

cone

2 Listen again.

🎧 **G** *Do you hear U?*

1 Listen. Mark Yes or No.

	Yes	No
1.	✓	
2.		✓
3.	✓	
4.	✓	
5.		✓
6.	✓	

U

cube

2 Listen again.

Unit 1 • **3**

🎧 **E** *Do you hear I?*

Audio script

1. ice	/aɪs/
2. tie	/taɪ/
3. say	/seɪ/
4. hi	/haɪ/
5. fries	/fraɪz/
6. cheese	/tʃiːz/

🎧 **F** *Do you hear O?*

Audio script

1. cone	/koʊn/
2. so	/soʊ/
3. go	/goʊ/
4. cake	/keɪk/
5. boat	/boʊt/
6. fries	/fraɪz/

🎧 **G** *Do you hear U?*

Audio script

1. cube	/kjuːb/
2. me	/miː/
3. cute	/kjuːt/
4. use	/juːz/
5. cone	/koʊn/
6. juice	/dʒuːs/

🎧 H Which word is different?

To introduce students to this type of exercise, practice it on the board. Write the letters X, Y, and Z with two rows of answer blanks underneath them. Say a set of three words (for example, *cake, cake, tea*) and point to the blanks under the X, Y, and Z as you say them. Have a student put a checkmark under the correct letter for the word that was different (in this case, under Z for the word *tea*). Give another example such as *ice, cone, ice*. Then proceed with the task.

Audio script

1. see, see, say
   /siː/, /siː/, /seɪ/

2. tea, tea, tie
   /tiː/, /tiː/, /taɪ/

3. me, my, me
   /miː/, /maɪ/, /miː/

4. way, we, way
   /weɪ/, /wiː/, /weɪ/

5. plays, please, plays
   /pleɪz/, /pliːz/, /pleɪz/

6. so, so, say
   /soʊ/, /soʊ/, /seɪ/

7. two, toe, two
   /tuː/, /toʊ/, /tuː/

8. why, we, why
   /waɪ/, /wiː/, /waɪ/

🎧 I Saying the alphabet vowels

Students will first hear the name of the letter and then the sound. For these letters, the two will sound exactly the same.

The shape (rounding or spreading) of the lips and the timing of this movement are crucial to pronouncing these vowels clearly. If you look at a Spanish-speaker's mouth just about to say *sí* /si/, the lips will be spread before the sound /s/ is begun. An English-speaker's mouth, just about to say *see* /siː/, will not spread the lips until the end of the /iː/ vowel, or the part of the vowel known as the "^{y} off-glide."

Tell students to smile when they say vowels that end in a ^{y} off-glide. Many other languages (e.g., Spanish and Japanese) do not have ^{y} or ^{w} off-glide endings for vowels, so it is a foreign concept to many students.

Note: Traditionally, I^y/aɪ/ is not classed as a diphthong (in which the tongue moves into two vowel positions), but the tongue does move a bit and the lips do end in a wide position. Grouping these three vowels together helps students learn the alphabet names of the vowel letters.

🎧 H Which word is different?

1 Listen to three words. One word is different. Mark it.

	X	Y	Z	
1.			✓	(see, see, say)
2.			✓	
3.		✓		
4.		✓		
5.		✓		
6.			✓	
7.		✓		
8.		✓		

2 Listen again.

🎧 I Saying the alphabet vowels

Listen. Say each sound two times.

Letter	Sound
A	A^y
E	E^y
I	I^y

At the end of the sound the lips are wide.

O	O^w
U	U^w

At the end of the sound the lips are round.

4 • Unit 1

🎧 **J** *Key words for the alphabet vowels*

1 Listen. Say each key word two times.

Letter	Sound	Key word	
A	A^y	cake	
E	E^y	tea	
I	I^y	ice	
O	O^w	cone	
U	U^w	cube	

2 Write the key words.

Letter	Key word
A	*cake*
E	*tea*
I	*ice*
O	*cone*
U	*cube*

Unit 1 • **5**

🎧 **J** **Key words for the alphabet vowels**

Key words help students remember the sound quality of these vowels, so these same key words will be repeated frequently throughout the early units. Food words are used as a main topic in the early units of this book because food is a popular subject and many students will already know some of this vocabulary.

Teaching Tip

To help reinforce the vowel sounds in the key words, make a chart of the vowels and key words and display it in the classroom. Students might like to make their own personal charts. As students progress through the course, they can add other words that have similar sounds.

🎧 **K** *Food*

Before listening, point to the pictures and say the words for your students, for example, *Fastburger, cheeseburger, French fries*, etc.

🎧 **L** **Music of English**

Throughout the book, *Music of English* tasks teach students the rhythm and intonation of English (or the music of the language). Students need to hear these sentences several times to get an accurate acoustic imprint in their minds before they are asked to speak. Either use the audio program or model the sentences yourself. If you model, be sure to lengthen the vowel sounds in *cake* and *tea* to introduce students to this aspect of English rhythm: The stressed syllable in the most important word in a sentence has a lengthened vowel. Then ask the class to say the words with you as you speak. If they "mirror" in this way (speaking in unison with the model), they will be absorbing the music of the language accurately.

Speaking in unison (as a chorus) is very supportive of correct musical patterns and also lowers the tension students feel when required to recite alone. An added benefit of "musical" recitation is that students can be more successful at achieving the target sounds if they are spoken with the proper timing (the target rhythm).

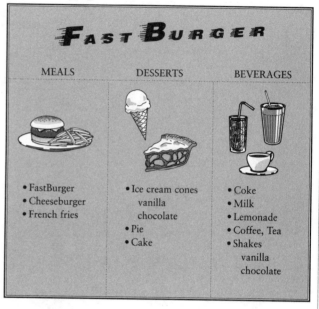

🎧 **K** ___Food___

Listen. Say each food two times.

FASTBURGER

MEALS	DESSERTS	BEVERAGES
• FastBurger	• Ice cream cones	• Coke
• Cheeseburger	vanilla	• Milk
• French fries	chocolate	• Lemonade
	• Pie	• Coffee, Tea
	• Cake	• Shakes
		vanilla
		chocolate

🎧 **L** **Music of English** ♩♪

Listen. Say each sentence two times.

Cake, please.

Tea, please.

6 • Unit 1

💡 *Teaching Tip*

Here is an interesting "saturation" method used by a teacher of Swedish pronunciation, Olle Kjellin, M.D., to help his students learn the rhythm of their new language. Ask your students to listen without saying anything as you repeat a sample sentence aloud ten to fifteen times. As you repeat, gradually exaggerate your body movements more each time to accompany and reinforce the rhythm and stress. Finally, ask the whole class to say the sentence in chorus with you, mirroring your speech, and repeating many times.

See Unit 1 Quiz on page T-131.

2 The Two Vowel Rule

How do you spell "time"?

🎧 A Saying the letters of the alphabet

Listen. Say the names of the letters and the key words.

Letter	Key words for vowels
A	cake
B	
C	
D	
E	tea
F	
G	
H	
I	ice
J	
K	
L	
M	
N	
O	cone
P	
Q	
R	
S	
T	
U	cube
V	
W	
X	
Y	
Z	

Unit 2 • 7

---

plenty of attention. This is because spelling aloud is such a useful tool for correcting misunderstandings. Even advanced students may be uncertain about the names of certain letters. Here are some that are confusing:

Letter	Name
a	/eɪ/
e	/iː/
i	/aɪ/
g	/dʒiː/
j	/dʒeɪ/

Sometimes students simply avoid saying difficult letters such as *w* /ˈdʌ•bəl•juː/, *x* /eks/, and *y* /waɪ/.

💡 Teaching Tip

For additional work with alphabet letters, students can copy the alphabet onto index cards to give to another student to arrange in order. (This guarantees they will try to write neatly.)

Sequencing the letters is a difficult task, even for students whose first language uses a Roman alphabet. Even though the letters may look familiar, they may be in a different order or have a different sound in a student's first language. These kinds of differences can make the use of a dictionary frustrating for learners, so it is important for students to learn the English alphabet early on.

---

2 The Two Vowel Rule

Unit overview

In this unit, students practice saying the alphabet sounds they listened to in Unit 1. Then they learn the Two Vowel Rule, which will help them guess how to pronounce words with two vowel letters.

🎧 A Saying the letters of the alphabet

In this task, learners repeat the letters of the alphabet. Most language courses begin with a brief presentation of the alphabet, and then move on quickly to other topics. However, learning to understand and say the names of the letters are important skills that merit

🎧 B *The Two Vowel Rule*

This task introduces a simple decoding rule that will help students figure out how a particular spelling might be pronounced. According to the Two Vowel Rule, when there are two vowel letters in a word, the first vowel letter says its alphabet name, and the second letter is silent.

There are exceptions to this rule, but it is true often enough to help students overcome the feeling that English spelling is an insurmountable obstacle. See Appendix E in the Student's Book for statistics on how often the rule works. For reference, here are some of the exceptions:

1. Sometimes the letters *y* and *w* act like vowels. When these letters immediately follow another vowel within a syllable, they activate the Two Vowel Rule.

   A^y   pay, say, play, stay
   O^w show, slow, grow, bowl

2. The letter *y* sometimes sounds like I^y /aɪ/: *shy, why, try, my, apply, type*. The letter *y* can also sound like E^y /iː/: *city, pretty, soapy, sunny, company*.

3. The Two Vowel Rule does not work for the vowel combinations *-au-*, *-ou-*, or *-oi-*, as in *auto*, *out*, and *oil*.

After students have listened to the words in step 1, write *make* on the board. Read the direction line in step 2 and model circling the first vowel. Then have students complete the task.

For step 3, read the rule aloud to the students. Then have them identify the first and second vowels in each of the key words in the box and practice saying the key words with you.

🎧 C **Words that end in the vowel letter *-e***

Tasks C and D demonstrate two different applications of the Two Vowel Rule. In this task, students see how the rule applies when the second vowel is a final *-e*. In the words in D the two vowel letters are next to each other, and the vowels vary.

🎧 B *The Two Vowel Rule*

1 Listen. Say each word two times.

2 Circle the first vowel letter in each word.

1. m(a)ke
2. r(i)ce
3. t(e)a
4. p(ie)
5. h(o)me
6. c(u)be
7. s(o)ap
8. (u)se

3 Read this rule.

> **The Two Vowel Rule**
>
> When there are two vowel letters in a word:
> 1. The first vowel says its alphabet name.
> 2. The second vowel is silent.
>
> This rule is true for many words.
>
>   cake   tea   ice   cone   cube

🎧 C **Words that end in the vowel letter *-e***

Listen. Say each word two times.

A^y	E^y	I^y	O^w	U^w
cake	Pete	ice	Coke	use
bake	see	rice	cone	cube
make	three	time	those	June
came	these	nine	home	rule
same	please	like	nose	cute

D Words with two vowel letters together

Listen. Say each word two times.

A^y	E^y	I^y	O^w	U^w
rain	eat	pie	boat	cue
train	meat	tie	Joe	suit
paid	read	fries	soap	fruit
wait	see	cries	coat	

E Which vowel letter says its name?

1 For each word, circle the vowel letter that says its name.

1. m(a)de p(ai)d n(a)me ch(a)nge c(a)ke J(a)ne J(a)ke
2. cr(ea)m pl(ea)se s(ee) ch(ee)se thr(ee) P(e)te
3. t(i)me s(i)ze r(i)ce l(i)ke wr(i)te b(i)ke M(i)ke
4. C(o)ke c(o)ne b(oa)t sm(o)ke J(oe)
5. c(u)te c(u)be tr(ue) fr(ui)t S(ue)

2 Check your answers with the class.

F Which vowel sound is it?

1 Listen. Say each word two times.

meat	meal	came	made	mine
see	soap	close	cue	cute
like	cheese	mile	rain	boat

2 Write each word in the correct box.

A^y cake	E^y tea	I^y ice	O^w cone	U^w cube
made	meat	mine	soap	cue
came	see	like	close	cute
rain	meal	mile	boat	
	cheese			

3 Listen again.

Unit 2 • 9

Teaching Tip

For extra practice, choose familiar one-syllable "classroom" words that follow the Two Vowel Rule and write them on the board. Have students identify the vowel letter that says its name. For example:

close	speak	write
white	read	note
chair	page	tape
time	rule	

Note: Many classroom words do not have two vowels. In Unit 4, students will learn about the One Vowel Rule, which covers classroom words such as the following:

class	pen	pencil
desk	window	listen
ask	task	
example	clock	

F Which vowel sound is it?

Here students practice discriminating between the five alphabet vowel sounds. If students need help getting started on step 2, copy the chart and vowel letters onto the board. Do several of the words as a class before students work individually.

D Words with two vowel letters together

This task helps to solidify students' understanding of the term *vowel letter*. As they listen, they should focus their attention on the first vowel letter, the one that most often determines the pronunciation of the word.

Note: When the letter *u* is the first of two vowel letters in a word, it can be pronounced either as ^{y}U^w /juː/ as in *cue*, or U^w /uː/ as in *suit*. However, the distinction is too subtle for beginners to try to master, and should not be taught at this point.

E Which vowel letter says its name?

To warm up, write several of the words on the board. Have students come up and circle the first vowel letter and pronounce the word. Then have students do the task individually.

🎧 G *Music of English*

The kind of exact musical repetition used in *Music of English* tasks takes advantage of the fact that people can remember the words, timing, and melodic pattern of a song or part of a song, even if they couldn't put them together correctly in a spoken sentence. Alternative pitch patterns are possible for almost all English sentences, but these "music boxes" will present a musical pattern that will be easily understood.

When you model these sentences for your students, be sure to lengthen the vowel in *time* and when you say the letter *e*. This will make a good model of the rhythm as well as the melody.

Note: After students listen to the audio program and repeat the sentences, have them repeat the exchange at least once more as a whole piece, to show how the meanings of the sentences are linked.

💡 *Teaching Tip*

Following the pitch line with your hand is a good kinesthetic reinforcement of the intonation pattern. With your hand, model the rise and fall of the pitch lines as you say the sentences. Then have students do it with you several times. This method can be used throughout the book.

🎧 H *Pair work: Asking how to spell words*

Spelling aloud (saying the names of the letters) is an important skill for students who have trouble being understood.

🎧 **G** Music of English 🎵♪

Listen. Say each sentence two times.

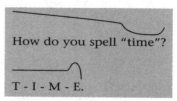

How do you spell "time"?

T - I - M - E.

🎧 **H** *Pair work: Asking how to spell words*

1 Listen.

2 Say the conversations with a partner.

Student A: How do you spell "same"?
Student B: S - A - M - E.
Student A: Right.

Student B: How do you spell "cone"?
Student A: C - A - N - E.
Student B: No, it's C - O - N - E.

I *Pair work: How do you spell "cheese"?*

1 Student A, ask how to spell a word from the Words box on the next page.

2 Student B, spell the word.

3 Take turns asking questions.

Examples

Student A: How do you spell "cheese"?
Student B: C - H - E - E - S - E.
Student A: Right.

cheese

Student B: How do you spell "tree"?
Student A: T - E - A.
Student B: No, it's T - R - E - E.

That is why practicing these questions and answers is so important. They will be used in exercises throughout this book.

When spelling aloud, each letter is like a separate syllable, and the final syllable of a series generally has a rise/fall intonation, to signify "end of list." To model this, write several words on the board. Spell each word with a rise/fall intonation on the last letter and then have the students repeat it with you.

▮ *Pair work: How do you spell "cheese"?*

Pair work practice keeps everybody in the class working, either concentrating on saying the sentence correctly or hearing it accurately. This sort of practice also lets them focus on each other, instead of the teacher, which lowers the tension involved in speaking. Circulate around the room to check on students' work.

Words

sale	same	take	cake	page
tea	tree	cheese	please	each
ice	size	rice	time	fries
close	hope	cone	coat	soap
cute	use	cube		

J Spelling game [EXTRA]

1 Divide into Team A and Team B.

2 Team A student, say the number and letter of a word from the box below.

3 Team B student, spell and pronounce the word.

4 Teams take turns asking questions.

5 Teams get one point for each correct answer.

Examples

Team A student: E-4
Team B student: S - H - A - K - E. Shake.

Team B student: B-3
Team A student: P - E - T - E. Pete.

	1	2	3	4	5
A	made	name	Mike	Jane	pie
B	please	sale	Pete	team	page
C	cute	cheese	June	write	each
D	change	ice	boat	time	fries
E	cake	rice	cone	shake	soap

grid should have letters down one side and numbers across the top. Students take turns challenging the other team by saying a letter and number combination, such as *E-4*. A student from the other team must spell the word in that cell of the grid and then pronounce it. One point can be given for every correct answer, or one point each can be awarded for correct spelling and correct pronunciation.

Teaching Tip

This spelling game can be used often during the course to review and reinforce what students are learning. Set up a grid in the same way and place new words in the cells.

See Unit 2 Quiz on page T-132.

After reading the directions, model the task. Take the part of Student A and choose someone in the class to take the part of Student B. Act out choosing a word from the box (without Student B seeing you point) and asking the question. Have Student B answer your question, and then ask you a question.

When doing the task, both students should look at the list. Try to have them concentrate on accurate pronunciation, rather than spelling from memory. Make sure the students choose words at random, rather than going down the columns in order. A random approach keeps the listening partner alert. Students may benefit by trying the exercise with more than one partner.

J Spelling game [EXTRA]

Copy the grid onto the board or an overhead transparency. The

3 Syllables

Unit overview

Unit 3 focuses students' attention on syllables. Students learn to listen to syllables, tap them out, and finally to count them. This lays the foundation for later units in which students will learn to identify the strong and weak syllables in words and phrases (Units 5 and 6, respectively).

Syllable number is an important topic because English learners often add or drop syllables according to the rules of their first language. This can cause serious intelligibility problems when, for example, *school* becomes "eschool" or "sekolah," *government* becomes "gahment," or *Yesterday I rented an apartment* becomes "Yest'day I rent' 'partment."

🎧 A Syllables

Before starting, point to the pictures and say the words *cheeseburger, milkshake,* and *banana.* Then clap or tap out the syllables as you say them again. As you go through each unit, remember to use the art to introduce or reinforce vocabulary.

If students want a definition of *syllable,* you can say that each syllable has a vowel sound in its center. However, this is a complicated abstraction, so it is better to teach *syllable* kinesthetically, as a physical sensation, like a beat or tap.

---

3 Syllables

How many syllables are in "city"?

🎧 A Syllables ☐☐☐

1 A syllable is a small part of a word. Listen.

cake	burger	cheeseburger
☐	☐ ☐	☐ ☐ ☐

2 Listen to the syllables in these words.

shake	milkshake	banana	banana milkshake
☐	☐ ☐	☐ ☐ ☐	☐ ☐ ☐ ☐ ☐

🎧 B Tapping the syllables ☐☐☐

Listen. Tap one time for each syllable.

☞	☞	☞	☞	☞
☐	☐ ☐	☐ ☐ ☐	☐ ☐ ☐ ☐	☐ ☐ ☐ ☐ ☐
shake	chocolate	vanilla	chocolate milkshake	vanilla milkshake
Coke	ice cream	cheese sandwich	turkey sandwich	banana milkshake
tea	iced tea	tomato	banana pie	potato salad
cheese	burger	cucumber	baked potato	tomato salad
pie	salad	lemonade		

🎧 B Tapping the syllables

After students listen to each word, have them tap out the syllables they heard. By tapping out the syllables, students feel the physical sensation of the rhythm and succession of syllables. If they are reluctant to tap with their fingers while counting syllables, they can be encouraged to count by tapping a foot or simply by touching thumb to fingers.

Some speakers pronounce *chocolate* /ˈtʃɑk•lət/ (or /ˈtʃɔːk•lət/), with three syllables (/ˈtʃɑk•ə•lət/), but the most common pronunciation in American English is with two syllables. Many other languages use four syllables for this word.

C *Which word is different?*

1 Listen to three words. One word is different. Mark it.

	X	Y	Z	
1.			✓	(sit, sit, city)
2.		✓		
3.			✓	
4.			✓	
5.		✓		
6.			✓	
7.			✓	
8.		✓		
9.			✓	
10.		✓		

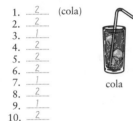
city

2 Listen again.

D *Counting syllables* ☐ ☐ ☐

1 Listen. Write the number of syllables you hear.

1. _2_ (cola)
2. _2_
3. _1_
4. _2_
5. _2_
6. _2_
7. _1_
8. _2_
9. _1_
10. _2_

cola

2 Listen again.

C *Which word is different?*

Here students listen for syllable number to determine which word is different. Students were introduced to this format in Unit 1, task H, but it may be helpful to review how it is done. Read the direction line and the three words shown next to item 1, the example. Draw attention to the checkmark in column Z. Then start the audio program or read the script.

Audio script

1. sit, sit, city
/sɪt/, /sɪt/, /ˈsɪt̬•i/

2. pep, pepsi, pep
/pep/, /ˈpep•si/, /pep/

3. icy, icy, ice
/ˈɑɪ•si/, /ˈɑɪ•si/, /ɑɪs/

4. cream, cream, creamy
/kriːm/, /kriːm/, /ˈkriː•mi/

5. cola, coal, cola
/ˈkoʊ•lə/, /koʊl/, /ˈkoʊ•lə/

6. shake, shake, shaker
/ʃeɪk/, /ʃeɪk/, /ˈʃeɪ•kər/

7. soap, soap, soapy
/soʊp/, /soʊp/, /ˈsoʊ•pi/

8. lemon, lemonade, lemon
/ˈle•mən/, /ˌlem•ə'neɪd/, /ˈle•mən/

9. cues, cues, excuse
/kjuːz/, /kjuːz/, /ɪkˈskjuːz/

10. six, sixty, six
/sɪks/, /ˈsɪk•st̬i/, /sɪks/

D *Counting syllables*

Because the rhythm of our speech is deeply connected to our sense of who we are and what group we belong to, students are sometimes uneasy about working on rhythm. A relaxed class atmosphere can help reduce this uneasiness. In some classes, students enjoy "dancing" exercises, where they can stand up and move various parts of the body (hand, head, foot, elbow, knee, etc.) to help count syllables.

Audio script

1. cola	/ˈkoʊ•lə/
2. city	/ˈsɪ•t̬i/
3. cream	/kriːm/
4. creamy	/ˈkriː•mi/
5. ice cream	/ˈɑɪs kriːm/
6. salad	/ˈsæl•əd/
7. cheese	/tʃiːz/
8. cheeses	/ˈtʃiːz•əz/
9. six	/sɪks/
10. sixty	/ˈsɪk•st̬i/

E Pair work: One or two syllables?

It is important to prepare students for pair work by going over the instructions and doing the examples with them. As students work in pairs, move around the class and help as needed. After students have finished, call out words from the task and have students hold up their fingers for the number of syllables.

Syllable counting is important not only for saying words clearly, but for grammatical accuracy. The syllables that students tend to leave out of their speech and writing are often grammatical markers (-ing, -ed, is, to, the, etc.). These small but important elements are hard to hear in spoken English because they are systematically said less clearly in natural speech. Increased awareness of syllable count can serve as a reminder to include these small words and word endings.

💡 Teaching Tip

Dictation is an excellent technique for checking your students' accuracy in listening. Ask them to close their books, and then dictate a series of words from this list, scrambling the order given in the Student's Book. Then check their writing or have them check each other's accuracy. This will verify that they are actually paying attention to the number of syllables. After some continued work with syllable number, use dictation to check again (perhaps at the end of this unit).

E Pair work: One or two syllables? ☐ ☐ ☐

1 Student A, say word **a** or word **b**.

2 Student B, hold up one or two fingers.

3 Take turns saying the words below.

Examples

> Student A: Ninety.
> Student B: (Hold up two fingers.)   ✌️
>
> Student B: Eight.
> Student A: (Hold up one finger.)   ☝️

1. a. ninety b. nine	6. a. rented b. rent
2. a. eighty b. eight	7. a. store b. a store
3. a. four b. forty	8. a. sit b. city
4. a. sixty b. six	9. a. blow b. below
5. a. rain b. raining	10. a. cleaned b. clean it

🎧 F Tapping syllables in words ☞

1 Listen.

2 Cover the words. Listen again. Say each word and tap the syllables.

3 Write the number of syllables.

1. banana	1. __3__
2. sandwich	2. __2__
3. milkshake	3. __2__
4. painted	4. __2__
5. rented	5. __2__
6. closed	6. __1__
7. opened	7. __2__
8. cleaned	8. __1__

🎧 F Tapping syllables in words

Here students listen to a list of words two times. The second time they listen, they should cover the list of words and tap out the syllables of each word after they hear it. Then have them write the number of syllables.

To check their work at the end, have students give the answer and then tap out the syllables as they say the word.

💡 Teaching Tip

Ask students how many syllables are in a word each time you introduce a new vocabulary item. This seems to help both spelling and memory of pronunciation.

G Tapping syllables in groups of words

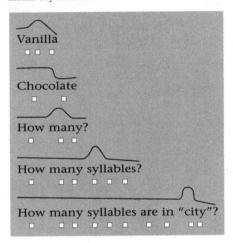

Listen. Say each group of words and tap the syllables.

1. a cheeseburger
2. a vanilla milkshake
3. a cheeseburger and fries
4. cheesecake and coffee
5. pie or ice cream
6. two salads and one milk

H Music of English ♫♪

Listen. Say each line two times.

Vanilla
☐ ☐ ☐

Chocolate
☐ ☐ ☐

How many?
☐ ☐ ☐

How many syllables?
☐ ☐ ☐ ☐

How many syllables are in "city"?
☐ ☐ ☐ ☐ ☐ ☐ ☐ ☐☐

Unit 3 • **15**

How many? /haʊ ˈme•ni/
How many syllables?
    /haʊ ˈme•ni ˈsɪl•ə•bəlz/
How many syllables are in city?
    /haʊ ˈme•ni ˈsɪl•ə•bəlz ər ɪn
    ˈsɪ•t̬i/

How many syllables are in "city"? is a very long sentence for beginners, containing ten syllables and including the difficult word *syllables*. If students try to recite this whole sentence, they are apt to become more and more uncertain as they move forward. You can help them master this sentence by using the technique of "backward buildup." Have students work on *in "city"?* first, concentrating on correct rhythm and melody in this phrase alone. Then work on *are in "city"?* When they can say this with confidence, lengthen it to *syllables are in "city"?* When these seven syllables are said easily and correctly, lengthen it to *How many syllables are in "city"?* At each step, the students are reciting in the direction of greater confidence.

💡 Teaching Tip

To vary the task, students can practice this musical exercise individually, in groups, or as a class. It is also helpful for students to follow the pitch line either by tracing the line in the book with their finger, or by drawing the pitch line in the air as they speak.

G Tapping syllables in groups of words

In this task, students progress to listening to and tapping out syllables in phrases.

After they hear each phrase on the audio program, they should repeat it while tapping out the syllables.

H Music of English

When you model these sentences (or lead students to say them in unison with the audio program) be sure to lengthen the stressed vowels:

vanilla /vəˈnɪ•lə/
chocolate /ˈtʃɔːk•lət/

I Pair work: How many syllables are in "forty"?

Warm up for the task by doing the examples with the class. After pair work, have individual students ask and answer questions for the class.

J The Two Vowel Rule for syllables

The Two Vowel Rule is repeated here, but *word* has been changed to *syllable*. This is to help students realize that the rule works for words with more than one syllable. Again, there are many exceptions, but the rule works well enough to serve as a useful guide for beginners, giving them more confidence in decoding English spelling.

Teaching Tip

Here are some more challenging words for additional practice. Write the words in columns on the board and have students repeat them after you. Have students come to the board and underline the syllable with two vowels, and circle the first vowel.

A^y

waitress /'weɪ•trəs/
arrangement /ə'reɪndʒ•mənt/

E^y

teacher /'tiː•tʃər/
easy /'iː•zi/

I^y

alive /ə'laɪv/
decide /dɪ'saɪd/
advice /əd'vaɪs/

O^w

telephone /'tel•ə,foʊn/
oatmeal /'oʊt•miːl/

U^w

avenue /'æv•ə,nuː/
continue /kən'tɪn•juː/
Tuesday /'tuːz•di/ or /'tuːz•deɪ/

I Pair work: How many syllables are in "forty"? □ □ □

1 Student A, choose a word from the list below. Ask how many syllables are in the word.

2 Student B, hold up one, two, or three fingers.

3 Take turns asking questions.

Examples

Student A: How many syllables are in "forty"?
Student B: (Hold up two fingers.)

Student B: How many syllables are in "vanilla"?
Student A: (Hold up three fingers.)

city	a city	salad	burger	store
forty	computer	a class	forty pies	coffee
class	vanilla	milkshake	cucumber	ice cream cone

J The Two Vowel Rule for syllables

1 Read the rule.

> **The Two Vowel Rule**
>
> When there are two vowel letters in a SYLLABLE:
>
> 1. The first vowel says its alphabet name.
> 2. The second vowel is silent.
>
> This rule is true for many words.
>
> | | | | | |
> |---|---|---|---|---|
> | cake | tea | ice | cone | cube |
> | remain | repeat | arrive | soapy | juice |

2 Listen. Say each word two times.

A^y	E^y	I^y	O^w	U^w
rain	please	wife	road	true
explain	repeat	mine	soap	juice
remain	complete	arrive	soapy	excuse

K Pair work: How do you spell "city"?

1 Student A, ask question **a** or **b**.

2 Student B, answer.

3 Take turns asking questions.

Examples

> Student A: How do you spell "sit"?
> Student B: S - I - T.
>
> Student B: How do you spell "forty"?
> Student A: F - O - U - R.
> Student B: No, it's F - O - R - T - Y.

1. a. How do you spell "city"?   C - I - T - Y.
   b. How do you spell "sit"?   S - I - T.

2. a. How do you spell "four"?   F - O - U - R.
   b. How do you spell "forty"?   F - O - R - T - Y.

3. a. How do you spell "raining"? R - A - I - N - I - N - G.
   b. How do you spell "rain"?   R - A - I - N.

4. a. How do you spell "rent"?   R - E - N - T.
   b. How do you spell "rented"?   R - E - N - T - E - D.

5. a. How do you spell "six"?   S - I - X.
   b. How do you spell "sixty"?   S - I - X - T - Y.

6. a. How do you spell "store"?   S - T - O - R - E.
   b. How do you spell "a store"? A S - T - O - R - E.

7. a. How do you spell "seventy"? S - E - V - E - N - T - Y.
   b. How do you spell "seven"?   S - E - V - E - N.

8. a. How do you spell "soap"?   S - O - A - P.
   b. How do you spell "soapy"?   S - O - A - P - Y.

Unit 3 • **17**

K Pair work: How do you spell "city"?

This type of task provides lots of practice with the names of the letters and the useful skill of spelling aloud. Make sure students are not just asking questions **a** and **b** in sequence, as this provides little challenge for their partners.

If students are relatively advanced, have the answering student listen with the words covered up. Lower-level students may need to read both sentences to themselves first, so that they can understand the meaning of the alternate choices. Use the illustrations provided to help them understand the vocabulary.

The task should be as challenging as possible, within the ability of the students to succeed. This makes it like a game.

💡 Teaching Tip

It can increase the usefulness of pair work if students go through the task with more than one partner. This not only provides extra practice but helps them learn to adjust to variation in pronunciation, since everyone speaks a little differently.

L *Food game* EXTRA

If the teams have difficulty getting started, help them think of some food words as a class. Write them on the board and count the syllables.

For more practice after the game, here are some additional words to give students. Students can write the words in the correct columns on the board. To check spelling, have them ask you *How do you spell . . . ?*

salad	/ˈsæl•əd/
potato	/pəˈteɪ•t̬oʊ/
asparagus	/əsˈpær•ə•gəs/
peas	/piːz/
butter	/ˈbʌ•t̬ər/
tomato	/təˈmeɪ•t̬oʊ/
avocado	/ɑ•və•kɑ•doʊ/
corn	/kɔːrn/
spaghetti	/spəˈget̬•i/
grapes	/greɪps/
carrots	/ˈkær•əts/
cucumber	/ˈkjuː‚kʌm•bər/
eggs	/egz/
raisins	/ˈreɪ•zənz/
toast	/toʊst/
chicken	/ˈtʃɪk•ən/
cheeseburger	/ˈtʃiːz‚bər•gər/
beef	/biːf/
tuna	/ˈtuː•nə/
mayonnaise	/ˈmeɪ•ə‚neɪz/
fish	/fɪʃ/
muffin	/ˈmʌf•ən/
celery	/ˈsel•ə•ri/
beans	/biːnz/
melons	/ˈmel•ənz/

See Unit 3 Quiz on page T-133.

9. a. How do you spell "painted"? P - A - I - N - T - E - D.
   b. How do you spell "paint"? P - A - I - N - T.

10. a. How do you spell "salt"? S - A - L - T.
    b. How do you spell "salad"? S - A - L - A - D.

L *Food game* EXTRA

1 Divide into teams.

2 Each team thinks of food words and writes the words in the boxes.

3 After five minutes, compare your boxes. Each team gets one point for each syllable.

1 syllable □	2 syllables □□	3 syllables □□□	4 syllables □□□□
rice	ice cream	banana	macaroni

The One Vowel Rule
Linking with N

What does "less" mean?
How do you say L - E - A - S - E?

 A   *The Green family and the Two Vowel Rule*

1 This is a family tree. Listen to the names.

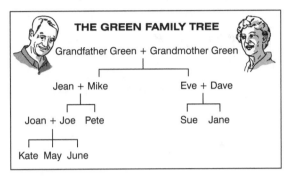

THE GREEN FAMILY TREE

Grandfather Green + Grandmother Green

Jean + Mike   Eve + Dave

Joan + Joe   Pete   Sue   Jane

Kate   May   June

2 In the Green family, all the names follow the Two Vowel Rule.

> **The Two Vowel Rule**
>
> When there are two vowel letters in a syllable:
>
> 1. The first vowel says its alphabet name.
> 2. The second vowel is silent.
>
> This rule is true for many words.
>
> | remain | repeat | arrive | soapy | excuse |
> |--------|--------|--------|-------|--------|
> | Jane | Jean | Mike | Joe | Sue |

Unit 4 • *19*

The One Vowel Rule
Linking with N

Unit overview

In Unit 4, students contrast the Two Vowel Rule they learned in Unit 2 with the One Vowel Rule. The unit also introduces the concept of *linking,* which is developed throughout the book. Linking, which refers to the way the final sound of a word connects to the initial sound of the word that follows it, is a key characteristic of spoken English. In this unit, learners listen to and practice words linked with *N* /n/, anticipating linking with *M* /m/ in Unit 5.

 A *The Green family and the Two Vowel Rule*

1. The purpose of this family tree is to introduce the idea of *relatives,* and to prepare students for learning the One Vowel Rule and the concept of a *relative vowel.* Students will hear sentences describing the relationships of people in the Green family. Students can point to the names as they hear them.

Audio script

> Grandfather Green and Grandmother Green
>
> Their children are Mike and Eve.
>
> Jean and Mike are married.
>
> Their children are Joe and Pete.
>
> Joe and Joan are married.
>
> Their children are Kate, May, and June.
>
> Eve and Dave are married.
>
> Their children are Sue and Jane.

2. Read the information in the box to remind students about the Two Vowel Rule.

Teaching Tip

The family trees in A and C could be put on the board or an overhead projector and used for practice with relationship terms (*sister, grandparents, children,* etc.).

As a good reminder of the One and Two Vowel Rules, put the family trees on posterboard and display them in the classroom for the remainder of the course.

T-19

🎧 **B** *Pair work: Questions about the Green family*

Make sure students know the gender of the names in the Green family so that they will know which people are sons, sisters, brothers, etc. Mike, Joe, Pete, and Dave are male, and the other names are female.

🎧 **C** *The Red family and the One Vowel Rule*

1. As students listen to the audio program for this exercise, they will focus on relative sounds. The term *relative sound* means that this sound is a relative of the *alphabet sound*. The alphabet sound and the relative sound are related because they are alternative pronunciations of the same vowel letter. The actual quality of a relative vowel sound must be learned by hearing it many times. Describing the position of the tongue is not as helpful as giving students opportunities to listen and develop an acoustic imprint in their minds.

The relative vowels are more common in spoken English than the alphabet vowels, but are more difficult for students to learn. That is why the Two Vowel Rule was presented first. Both of these rules have many exceptions, but they work well enough to help students decide how a printed word is likely to be pronounced. Some statistics about how often these rules work are given in Appendix E of the Student's Book.

Audio script

> Grandfather Red and
> Grandmother Red

B ___ *Pair work: Questions about the Green family*

Ask each other questions about the Green family. Write your answers.

1. Who is Joe's brother? .... *Pete*
2. Who is Jane's sister? .... *Sue*
3. Who is Eve's mother? .... *Grandmother Green*
4. Who is May's father? .... *Joe*
5. Who is Grandmother Green's son? .... *Mike*
6. Who are Kate's sisters? .... *May and June*
7. Who is Dave's wife? .... *Eve*
8. Who are Jean's sons? .... *Joe and Pete*

🎧 **C** ___ *The Red family and the One Vowel Rule*

1 This is the Red family. Listen.

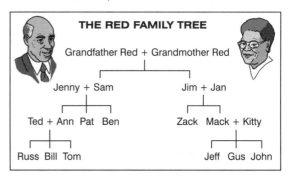

THE RED FAMILY TREE

Grandfather Red + Grandmother Red

Jenny + Sam   Jim + Jan

Ted + Ann Pat Ben   Zack Mack + Kitty

Russ Bill Tom   Jeff Gus John

2 In the Red family, all the names follow the One Vowel Rule.

> **The One Vowel Rule**
>
> When there is only one vowel letter in a syllable:
>
> 1. The vowel letter does NOT say its alphabet name.
> 2. The vowel letter says its RELATIVE sound.
>
> This rule is true for many words.
>
> | can | pencil | finger | hot | summer |
> |-----|--------|--------|-----|--------|
> | Mack | Jenny | Kitty | John | Russ |

Sam and Jim are their children.

Jenny and Sam are married.

Ann, Pat, and Ben are their children.

Ted and Ann are married.

Russ, Bill, and Tom are their children.

Jim and Jan are married.

Zack and Mack are their children.

Mack and Kitty are married.

Jeff, Gus, and John are their children.

2. Go over the One Vowel Rule with students. It can be helpful to tell them that very short words that end in a vowel do not follow this rule (e.g., *hi, me, she, go*).

Students may want to know the gender of the names. Pat could be either male or female. Jenny, Ann, Jan, and Kitty are females, and the other names are male.

D Words with relative vowel sounds

Listen.

A	E	I	O	U
Pat	Ben	Jim	Tom	Gus
hat	bed	his	hot	bus
Zack	pen	Bill	pot	sun
thanks	pencil	finish	John	sunny
Sam	Betty	Kitty	Johnny	supper

E Alphabet vowels and relative vowels

Alphabet vowels say their names. Relative vowels have a different sound.

1 These names have alphabet vowel sounds. Listen.

A^y	E^y	I^y	O^w	U^w
Jane	Jean	Mike	Joe	June

2 These names have relative vowel sounds. Listen.

A	E	I	O	U
Jan	Jen	Bill	Tom	Gus

F Which word is different?

1 Listen to three words. One word is different. Mark it.

	X	Y	Z	
1.		✓		(mate, mat, mate)
2.		✓		
3.	✓			
4.		✓		
5.	✓			
6.			✓	
7.		✓		

2 Listen again.

D Words with relative vowel sounds

In this exercise, students will hear relative vowel sounds. This book differs from the traditional approach to teaching vowel sounds in two ways:

1. Instead of using the terms *long* and *short* vowels, it refers to *alphabet* and *relative* vowels.

2. It groups pairs of likely sounds for the same vowel letters rather than in terms of their position in the mouth.

Many teachers use the terms *long* and *short* vowels. It is true that an alphabet vowel said by itself (out of context) sounds longer than a relative (short) vowel, simply because the alphabet vowels have a ^{y} or ^{w} off-glide that takes time to say. (Relative vowels do not have off-glides.) However, in the actual context of a word, short vowels can take longer to say than the long ones, because vowel length in English is largely determined by the presence or absence of other features, such as voicing in the following sound, and word or sentence stress. Therefore, in the context of whole words and sentences, *long* and *short* vowels are not very helpful terms.

It has been traditional to teach vowels in pairs based on their position within the mouth (e.g., /ɪ/ and /i/, as in *ship* and *sheep*), but this is not as useful for beginners as pairing the most likely sounds for the same vowel letter (e.g., *made* and *mad*, /meɪd/ and /mæd/).

For all of these reasons, this book uses the terms *long* and *short* to refer only to real timing length, when the vowels are said in actual running speech.

Note: The alphabet sound A^y has another relative sound, but it is less common: *all* /ɔːl/, *call, ball, mall, fall.*

E Alphabet vowels and relative vowels

Before students listen to the audio program, remind them to pay attention to the differences between the alphabet vowels and relative vowels they will hear.

F Which word is different?

Here students listen for vowel sounds to determine which word is different. Read the direction line and the three words shown next to item 1. Draw attention to the checkmark in column Y. Then start the audio program or read the script.

Audio script

1. mate, mat, mate
   /meɪt/, /mæt/, /meɪt/

2. pine, pin, pine
   /paɪn/, /pɪn/, /paɪn/

3. mean, men, men
   /miːn/, /men/, /men/

4. hop, hope, hop
   /hɑp/, /hoʊp/, /hɑp/

5. at, ate, ate
   /æt/, /eɪt/, /eɪt/

6. ice, ice, is
   /aɪs/, /aɪs/, /ɪz/

7. cute, cut, cute
   /kuːt/, /kʌt/, /kuːt/

G Listening to vowel sounds

Students often worry when they do not know the meaning of all the words they see, but try to get students to pay attention to the spelling, not the meaning, in this task. The purpose of this task is to help students learn to guess the vowel sounds by listening and looking at the spelling. Discussing vocabulary would use time better spent mastering the connection between sound and spelling.

H Which vowel sound do you hear?

1. As students listen to the audio program, they can put a checkmark next to the words they think have alphabet vowel sounds. This will help them when they do step 2 of the task.

2. Have students write the words in the correct boxes. They can do this in pairs or groups. Write the chart on the board and check answers as a class by asking, *What words go in this box?*

T-22

G Listening to vowel sounds

Listen. Point to each word as you hear it.

Aʸ	A	Eʸ	E	Iʸ	I	Oʷ	O	Uʷ	U
Kate	cat	teen	ten	ice	is	load	lot	cute	cut
Jane	Jan	Jean	Jen	file	fill	Joan	John	cube	cub
ate	at	meat	met	time	Tim	hope	hop	rule	run
same	Sam	seat	set	bite	bit	coat	cot	tube	tub

H Which vowel sound do you hear?

1 Listen. Some words have alphabet vowel sounds and some have relative vowel sounds.

cute	teen	rule	ride	pine	lease
made	road	main	cube	ice	coast
hop	shake	less	mad	rod	man
cheese	fun	chess	cub	shack	ten
rid	cut	hot	is	hope	pin

2 Write the words in the correct boxes. Each box has three words.

Aʸ	Eʸ	Iʸ	Oʷ	Uʷ
made	*cheese*	*ride*	*road*	*cute*
shake	*teen*	*pine*	*hope*	*rule*
main	*lease*	*ice*	*coast*	*cube*

A	E	I	O	U
mad	*less*	*rid*	*hop*	*fun*
shack	*chess*	*is*	*hot*	*cut*
man	*ten*	*pin*	*rod*	*cub*

3 Check your answers with the class.

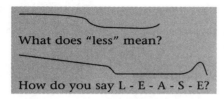

🎧 **I** ___Music of English___ 🎵♪

Listen. Say each sentence two times.

What does "less" mean?

How do you say L - E - A - S - E?

J ___Pair work: How do you say L-E-S-S?___

1 Student A, ask question **a** or **b**.

2 Student B, answer the question.

3 Take turns asking questions.

Examples

Student A: What does "less" mean?
Student B: Not as much.

Student B: How do you say S - H - A - K - E?
Student A: Shake.

1. a. What does "lease" mean?   To rent, usually for a year.
   b. What does "less" mean?   Not as much.

2. a. How do you say
      S - H - A - C - K?   Shack.
   b. How do you say
      S - H - A - K - E?   Shake.

3. a. What does "shake" mean?   A drink made of
                                   ice cream.
   b. What does "shack" mean?   A very poor house.

🎧 **I** *Music of English*

What does "less" mean? is another useful "song" for beginners. *How do you say L-E-A-S-E?* helps students gradually develop the skill of spelling aloud.

The letters in a spelled word are said like a series of any kind, and the signal for "last one" is a rise and then fall. This is also true for acronyms (e.g., *CNN, BBC, VIP,* etc.) and lists of any kind. When you model these sentences, lengthen the vowel sound in *less* and the final letter *-e* in *L-E-A-S-E*. *Less* and the final letter in *L-E-A-S-E* are the most important parts of these sentences, and as such they have longer vowels. Unit 5 will explain this for the students, but in the meantime they need to hear you say the sentences spoken with accurate English rhythm.

🔆 *Teaching Tip*

"Walkabout" is a useful technique: Have students circle the room, walking to the rhythm as they say the sentences many times. The teacher can step out of the circle and listen to the students as they go around. When students say the word *less,* they should take an extra long step. Then have students take a separate step for each letter of the word, *L-E-A-S-E,* with an extra long step for the final letter *-e.* For full effect, the walking/talking needs a lot of repetition.

J *Pair work: How do you say L-E-S-S?*

After reading the directions, ask students to read the examples. Then model the task by taking the part of Student A and choosing someone in the class to take the part of Student B. Act out choosing a question to ask, then have Student B answer your question. Confirm or correct the answer, then have Student B ask you a question. Finally, put students into pairs and have them take turns asking and answering the questions. Make sure students choose questions at random to keep the task interesting.

Short-form answers are given here, rather than full sentences, because that is how people actually talk. Also, short, easy-to-say responses are easier to produce and will help this sort of pair work go smoothly.

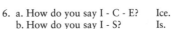

K Linking with the sound N

This exercise introduces students to the concept of linking. Many languages have a brief silence between all words, and in written English, words are separated with a white space. However, in spoken English, the final sound of a word often links to the initial sound of the next.

It is important to practice linking for two main reasons. First, listening comprehension is improved when students practice hearing words run together. Second, linking is an aid to fluency; when students link words in their own speech, they sound more natural and can begin to express themselves in thought groups, rather than in unnaturally separated words.

There are other good reasons for students to practice linking. Many languages do not allow final consonants, and students need practice concentrating on consonant endings.

Linking is also a good way to help students learn to pronounce difficult sounds, because it effectively moves word-final sounds into word-initial position. Often, students will have less trouble hearing and pronouncing a difficult sound at the beginning of a word than at the end.

1. When you model the linked words in this task, draw out the linking sound in an exaggerated way, to focus attention on the link.

2. Point out to students that the letter *k* is silent in *know*.

4. a. How do you say
      L - E - A - S - E?   Lease.
   b. How do you say
      L - E - S - S?   Less.

5. a. How do you spell "wheel"?   W - H - E - E - L.
   b. How do you spell "well"?   W - E - L - L.

6. a. How do you say I - C - E?   Ice.
   b. How do you say I - S?   Is.

7. a. How do you spell "while"?   W - H - I - L - E.
   b. How do you spell "will"?   W - I - L - L.

8. a. What does "main" mean?   The most important.
   b. What does "man" mean?   A male person.

9. a. How do you say
      C - H - E - S - S?   Chess.
   b. How do you say
      C - H - E - E - S - E?   Cheese.

10. a. What does "made" mean?   The past of "make."
    b. What does "mad" mean?   Angry.

K Linking with the sound N

Many words are linked together.

1 The sound N links to a vowel sound at the beginning of the next word. Listen.

Dan is.   Dannnis .

an apple   annnapple

2 The sound N links to another N sound at the beginning of the next word. Listen.

John knows.   Johnnnknows .

ten names   tennnnames

24 • Unit 4

T-24

🎧 **L** ___ **More linking with N** ⊂⊃⊂⊃⊂⊃⊂⊃⊂⊃

Listen. Say each sentence two times. Remember to link **N** to the sound at the beginning of the next word.

1. Dan is here.   Dannnis here.
2. Ken asks questions.   Kennnasks questions.
3. Jan and I will go.   Jannnand I will go.
4. Joan always goes.   Joannnalways goes.
5. Jean never goes.   Jeannnnever goes.
6. John knows everything.   Johnnnknows everything.
7. This is an ice cube.   This is annnice cube.
8. I want an apple.   I want annnapple .
9. The list has ten names.   The list has tennnnames .
10. Have you seen Nancy?   Have you seennnNancy ?

M ___ **Review: Names of the alphabet letters**

Say the names of the letters in each group. The letter names in each group have the same vowel sound. Read down.

A^y cake	E^y tea	E ten	I^y ice	O^w cone	U^w cube
A	B	F	I	O	U
H	C	L	Y		Q
J	D	M		W	
K	E	N			
	G	S			
	P	X			
	T				
	V				
	Z				

R does not belong in any of these groups. It is pronounced like the word "are."

Unit 4 • **25**

🎧 **L** *More linking with N*

This is the first task in which students actually have the opportunity to practice linking.

Students will hear sentences and repeat them at least two times. A useful approach is to have students use their index fingers to draw a linking symbol (like the curved line that connects *Dan* and *is* in item **1**) in the air as they say the linking *N* sound in each sentence. Encourage students to exaggerate the linking sounds as they practice.

Another approach is to instruct students to bring their hands together just as they begin the linking sound. This physical effort requires close attention to the onset of linking, which increases focus on the linking use of the target sound.

M **Review: Names of the alphabet letters**

This task is meant to help students pronounce these vowel sounds accurately, and at the same time, to reinforce work done in Units 1 and 2 on pronouncing the names of the letters.

💡 **Teaching Tip**

A more challenging task can be presented by writing the alphabet on the board and then asking students to cover up the columns in the book, except for the sounds and key words at the top of the chart. Then ask them to work in pairs or small teams, to figure out which letters go in which columns.

See Unit 4 Quiz on page T-134.

5 Strong syllables Linking with M

Unit overview

In this unit, students learn the rules for strong syllables. The terms *strong* and *weak* syllables are used to introduce students to the concept of *stressed* and *de-stressed* (or *reduced*) syllables because the terms *strong* and *weak* are less abstract. Learners practice lengthening the strong syllables in individual words and in the most important word of a sentence. Many other languages have relatively equal length for all syllables, and it is difficult for speakers of those languages to notice variable syllable length in English. Being aware of syllable length is important for understanding word and sentence stress patterns, an essential part of communication in spoken English.

Next, students focus on linking with *M* /m/, building on what they learned in Unit 4 about linking with *N* /n/. Finally, they listen for the *-ed* ending of verbs and practice distinguishing whether or not there is an extra syllable.

---

5 Strong syllables Linking with M

What's that called?
What's it for?

A Strong syllables

1 Listen.

1. Canada

   Ca**na**da

2. America

   A**me**rica

3. Australia

   Aus**tra**lia

4. Cambodia

   Cam**bo**dia

2 Read this rule.

> **The Strong Syllable Rule**
>
> When you say a word alone:
>
> 1. Each word has one strong syllable.
> 2. The vowel in a strong syllable is long.
>
> **pa**per   **pen**cil   com**pu**ter

3 Listen. Say this word two times.

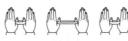

ba **na** na

A Strong syllables

1. Point out to students how the vowel letter at the center of one syllable is extra wide (stretched). This makes it easier for them to notice the extra length of the stressed syllable. Only the vowel is stretched because it is really just the core of a stressed syllable, or its vowel, that is lengthened. This lengthening is foreign to many learners, and therefore important to practice.

3. When you model the word *banana* for students, exaggerate the lengthened vowel so that students can hear it easily. Stretching a wide rubber band as they say the syllable, or just moving their hands apart, helps students develop a physical sense of this variable length. Using a rubber band also helps students get the idea of counting syllables, because they have to concentrate on when to stretch and when not to stretch.

Note: Use a wide rubber band. A thin rubber band does not convey the effort a student must make to adequately lengthen the vowel, and is also apt to break.

🎧 **B** **_Listening for strong syllables_**

1 Listen for the strong syllable in each word. Circle the long vowel in the strong syllable.

1. ban(a)na 5. van(i)lla
2. C(a)nada 6. ch(o)colate
3. fr(ee)zer 7. (e)lephant
4. bl(a)nket 8. Am(e)rica

2 Check your answers with the class.

🎧 **C** **_Saying strong syllables_**

Listen. Say each word two times. In the strong syllable, make the vowel long.

1. sofa

so fa

2. blanket

bla nket

3. carpet

ca rpet

4. newspaper

ne wspaper

5. telephone

te lephone

6. washing machine

wa shing machine

Unit 5 • **27**

Students of English tend not to notice word-stress patterns, or to assume that they are some sort of frill. Far from being frills, word-stress patterns are essential to clear communication in spoken English. A stress-pattern mistake can cause great confusion, especially if it is accompanied by any other kind of error, because it is hard for native speakers to understand words that are stressed incorrectly.

Note: When you check the answers and come to the word _chocolate,_ remind students of the importance of the number of syllables. In some languages, this word is pronounced with four syllables.

🎧 **C** **_Saying strong syllables_**

Have students repeat the words they hear. They can use a rubber band to show syllable length as they did in A.

Audio script

1. sofa
   /'soʊ•fə/
2. blanket
   /'blæŋ•kət/
3. carpet
   /'kɑr•pət/
4. newspaper
   /'nuːs,peɪ•pər/
5. telephone
   /'tel•ə,foʊn/
6. washing machine
   /'wɑ•ʃɪŋ•mə,ʃiːn/

   (continued)

🎧 **B** **_Listening for strong syllables_**

Students will listen for the strong (stressed) syllables in each word and circle the long vowel in that syllable. Some students may have difficulty noticing stress, especially if their first language has _fixed stress_ that always falls on the same syllable: often the first, or the next to last. Unfortunately for learners, English stress does not have a fixed location. Since there are no simple, practical rules for placement of stress, the most useful approach is to teach students to listen for the extra length and contrastive clarity of the stressed vowels. The shortness and obscurity of vowels in weak syllables (taught in the next unit) serve to contrastively highlight the length and clarity of stressed vowels in strong syllables.

7. refrigerator
/rɪˈfrɪdʒ•ə،reɪt̬•ər/

8. television
/ˈtel•ə،vɪʒ•en/

9. freezer
/ˈfriː•zər/

10. alarm clock
/əˈlɑrm،klɑk/

11. can opener
/ˈkæn،ou•pən•ər/

12. vacuum cleaner
/ˈvæk•juːm،kliː•nər/

13. ceiling
/ˈsiː•lɪŋ/

14. bathtub
/ˈbæθ•tʌb/

D Strong syllables in sentences

This task presents the rules for strong syllables in a sentence – probably the most important feature of English pronunciation taught in this course. The key rule is introduced in step 2 on page 29: *The vowel in the strong syllable of the important word is extra long.* When students learn to emphasize the most important word by lengthening the vowel in its strong syllable, they will have a major tool for improving the clarity of their English. This timing signal helps the listener to notice where the pitch is changed, and therefore to understand which word is most important. This will be explained to students in Unit 7, but the *Music of English* boxes in Units 5 and 6 will give them practice using vowel length correctly.

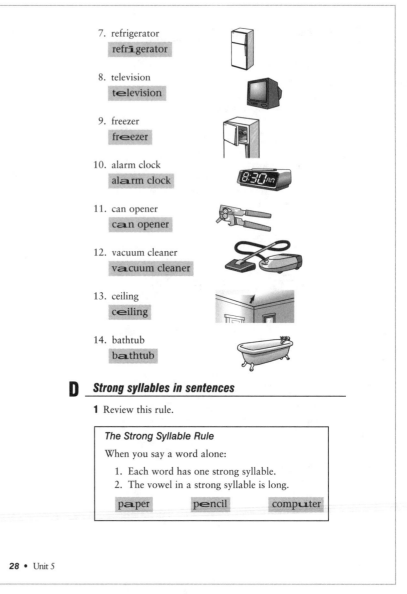

7. refrigerator
refri̱gerator

8. television
te̲levision

9. freezer
fre̲ezer

10. alarm clock
ala̲rm clock

11. can opener
ca̲n opener

12. vacuum cleaner
va̲cuum cleaner

13. ceiling
ce̲iling

14. bathtub
ba̲thtub

D Strong syllables in sentences

1 Review this rule.

> **The Strong Syllable Rule**
>
> When you say a word alone:
>
> 1. Each word has one strong syllable.
> 2. The vowel in a strong syllable is long.
>
> pa̲per   pe̲ncil   compu̲ter

28 • Unit 5

1. Review the Strong Syllable Rule with students. This rule applies to words in isolation.

2. Introduce the new rule, which pertains to words in sentences.

2 Read this new rule.

Another Strong Syllable Rule

When you say words in a SENTENCE:

1. One word is the most important.
2. The vowel in the strong syllable of the important word is extra long.

I need a pɘncil .   I nɘeded a pencil.

🎧 **E** **Music of English** 🎵🎶

Listen. Say each sentence two times.

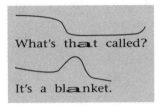

F **Pair work: What's that called?**

1 Student A, point to a picture on the next page and ask, "What's that called?"

2 Student B, say an answer from the Answers box.

3 Take turns asking questions.

Examples

Student A: (Point to picture of a blanket.) What's that called?
Student B: It's a blanket .

Student B: (Point to picture of a telephone.) What's that called?
Student A: It's a telephone .

🎧 **E** *Music of English*

Before students listen to the audio program, remind them that the stretched letters show them which vowels they should lengthen.

The contractions *What's* and *It's* are the usual form in spoken English (but not in formal written English).

Note: After students listen to the audio program and repeat the sentences, have them repeat the exchange at least once more as a whole piece, to show how the meanings and intonation patterns of the sentences are linked.

💡 *Teaching Tip*

A good way to practice contractions is to write on the board the following (or other auxiliary contractions):

I am	I'm
He is	He's
They will	They'll

Lead half the class to say the first word *(I)*, then lead the other half to say the second word *(am)*, and then have the whole class say them both together *(I'm)*. When done in a rhythmic chant, this is a powerful technique for practicing the difference in syllable number between the full, emphatic form and the more usual contracted form.

F *Pair work: What's that called?*

After reading the directions, model the task by taking the part of Student A and choosing someone in the class to take the part of Student B. It can be helpful to point to the pictures on page 30 and have the class say the names of the objects in unison. Then put students into pairs and have them take turns asking and answering the questions.

🎧 G *Music of English*

What's it for? is another useful fixed "song." The answer gives students good practice in noticing which word usually gets the emphasis.

Note: After students listen to the audio program and repeat the sentences, have them repeat the exchange at least once more as a whole piece, to show how the meanings and intonation patterns of the sentences are linked.

🎧 H *What's it for?*

Then have students listen to the audio program and repeat each sentence two times.

Note: Clothes (in item **10** on page 31) is usually pronounced just like *close* /kloʊz/, so there is no need for students to make an effort to say the *th* /ð/ part of the word.

Model one or two of these items to show students how the stretched vowels are lengthened and how these sentences follow the intonation pattern just practiced in G (*It's for keeping you warm.*) with a rise and fall on the most important word.

Answers

It's a telephone.	It's a can opener.
It's a sofa.	It's a blanket.
It's a washing machine.	It's an alarm clock.
It's a refrigerator.	It's a ceiling.
It's a vacuum cleaner.	It's a bathtub.

🎧 G *Music of English* 🎵🎶

Listen. Say each sentence two times.

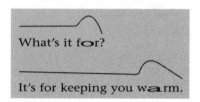

What's it for?

It's for keeping you warm.

🎧 H *What's it for?*

Listen. Say each sentence two times.

1. It's for calling people.
2. It's for keeping food cold .
3. It's for waking you up .
4. It's for opening cans .
5. It's for watching shows .
6. It's for reading the news .
7. It's for sitting on.

8. It's for cleaning the `carpet`.

9. It's for keeping you `warm`.

10. It's for washing `clothes`.

I Pair work: What's it for?

1 Student A, say a word from the Words box below. Ask, "What's it for?"

2 Student B, say an answer from the list in H on pages 30 and 31.

3 Take turns asking questions.

Examples

> Student A: `Television`. What's it `for`?
> Student B: It's for watching `shows`.
>
> Student B: `Newspaper`. What's it `for`?
> Student A: It's for reading the `news`.

Words

television	telephone	refrigerator	newspaper
blanket	sofa	can opener	alarm clock
washing machine	vacuum cleaner		

J Review: Counting syllables ☐ ☐ ☐

1 Say each word. Write the number of syllables.

1. Canada   3
2. sofa   2
3. blanket   2
4. telephone   3
5. paper towels   4
6. television   4
7. freezer   2
8. alarm clock   3
9. carpet   2
10. refrigerator   5

2 Check your answers with the class.

Unit 5 • *31*

J Review: Counting syllables

Have students write the number of syllables in the words. Then put the answers on the board so that they can check their work.

To extend the task, ask students to list some classroom items and count the syllables for those words. Here are some examples:

chalkboard	2
eraser	3
picture	2
map	1
backpack	2
women	2
men	1
window	2
dictionary	4
file cabinet	4

I Pair work: What's it for?

After reading the instructions, model the examples in the box with a student. Then put students into pairs and have them take turns asking and answering the question, *What's it for?* Remind them that all of the answers are in H.

For further practice, you can have students ask you about other items in the classroom. Write on the board, *What's this / that called?* and *What's it for?* to help them. Then students can point to items and ask these questions.

🎧 **K** **Linking with M**

Remind students that it is very important to practice linking because it will make their speech sound more natural and it will improve their listening comprehension. Explain that in normal English speech, words are run together rather than separated by silence.

Have students listen to the examples they hear in steps 1 and 2 and repeat the sentences they hear in step 3 at least two times. Encourage students to exaggerate the linking sounds as they practice and to draw a linking symbol (curved line) in the air as they say the linking *M* sound.

🎧 **L** **Past -ed ending**

Tasks L, M, and N, which focus on the past tense ending *-ed*, may be very useful for students who have begun to learn about this past tense form. However, the past tense ending may be too advanced for your students if they have not studied this tense yet. If this is the case, just ask them to count the syllables as they listen to tasks L and M, without going on to explain the rules for pronouncing the *-ed* ending. Then skip task N.

🎧 **K** **Linking with M** ⊂━⊂━⊂━⊂━⊃

1 The sound M links to a vowel sound at the beginning of the next word. Listen.

Jim is.	Jimmmis .
Come on.	Comemmon .

2 The sound M links to another M sound at the beginning of the next word. Listen.

Tom may.	Tommmmay .
some more	somemmmore

3 Listen. Say each sentence two times.

1. Jim is here. Jimmmis here.
2. What time is it? What timemmis it?
3. Sam and I will go. Sammmand will go.
4. We want some more. We want somemmmore
5. Ice cream is cold. Ice creammmis cold.
6. Tom may go home. Tommmmay go home.
7. Turn the alarm off. Turn the alarmmmoff .
8. She came much later. She camemmmuch later.

🎧 **L** **Past -ed ending**

1 Usually, -ed is added for the past form of a verb. Listen.

Present + -ed = Past

rent	rented
need	needed
play	played
talk	talked

2 Say each word two times. Tap the syllables.

🎧 M *Extra syllable or not?* ☐ ☐ ☐

Sometimes -ed makes an extra syllable. But usually it does not.

1 Listen.

Present + -ed = Past

| rent | rented |
| ☐ | ☐ ☐ |

| need | needed |
| ☐ | ☐ ☐ |

| talk | talked |
| ☐ | ☐ |

| wash | washed |
| ☐ | ☐ |

| listen | listened |
| ☐ ☐ | ☐ ☐ |

| plan | planned |
| ☐ | ☐ |

2 Listen. Hold up one finger if you hear one syllable. Hold up two fingers if you hear two syllables.

Final -t + -ed	Final -d + -ed	Other letters
painted	added	opened
rented	loaded	walked
counted	landed	cleaned
planted	needed	closed

3 Read these rules.

> **The Past Tense Syllable Rules**
>
> 1. When a verb ends with -t or -d, -ed will be an extra syllable.
> 2. When a verb ends in any other letter, -ed will NOT be an extra syllable.
>
> | add | added | close | closed |
> | ☐ | ☐ ☐ | ☐ | ☐ |

🎧 M *Extra syllable or not?*

This task helps students focus on whether they hear the past tense *-ed* as an extra syllable, or not, at the end of verbs. Step 3 introduces the rules that explain when the *-ed* ending adds an extra syllable.

Note: Point out that *talk* /tɔːk/ has a silent letter *l*.

💡 *Teaching Tip*

To reinforce the idea that sometimes the past tense *-ed* ending does not add an extra syllable, do an activity called "Vanishing Letters." On white poster board, write *closed*, *opened*, *washed*, and other past tense verbs with a "silent" *e* in the *-ed* ending. The words should be written in black except for the silent *e*, which should be written in yellow.

Show the list to the class, then cover it with a big piece of red acetate (transparent plastic sheeting). The yellow letters will disappear. Ask the class to read the words aloud as a chorus. The empty spaces act as reminders that although there is a letter *e* in the ending, it is not pronounced.

This makes a good visual display, but it is even better if students get the opportunity to do the writing themselves. For an interesting kinesthetic activity, give students a yellow marker, pencil, or crayon and a small square of red acetate. (Cut up pieces from a clear red report cover.) Then students can make their own lists on white paper. The word lists can be suggested by teams and can be extended to any kind of word with silent letters (e.g., *knife*, *knee*, *talk*, *walk*, etc.). When the lists are finished, they serve as scripts to practice pronouncing the words without the silent letters. The writing activity takes real focus, as it is not so easy to remember to put down the pen or pencil and pick up the yellow marker. You can collect the materials afterwards for later use.

N Pair work: Yesterday or every day?

This task gives students practice listening for and pronouncing the past tense *-ed* ending in the context of whole sentences. It also reinforces students' understanding of how meaning is connected to form.

After reading the instructions, model the examples in the box with a student. Then put students into pairs and have them take turns saying either sentence **a** or **b** and responding with *every day* or *yesterday*.

When they finish, you can consolidate by saying some additional sentences and having students respond as a whole class.

Examples

> We want a new car.
> He used a backpack.
> You washed the dishes.
> We brush our teeth.

See Unit 5 Quiz on page T-135.

---

4 Write -ed after these verbs. Then say each word two times.

Extra syllable	No extra syllable
1. want_ed_	8. rain_ed_
2. end_ed_	9. talk_ed_
3. add_ed_	10. wash_ed_
4. repeat_ed_	11. push_ed_
5. visit_ed_	12. look_ed_
6. wait_ed_	13. play_ed_
7. lift_ed_	14. call_ed_

N Pair work: Yesterday or every day?

1 Student A, say sentence **a** or **b**.

2 Student B, say "Every day" for present or "Yesterday" for past.

3 Take turns saying sentences.

Examples

> Student A: We plant flowers.
> Student B: Every day.
>
> Student B: We wanted a ride.
> Student A: Yesterday.

1. a. We planted flowers.
   b. We plant flowers.

2. a. We wanted a ride.
   b. We want a ride.

3. a. I need more money.
   b. I needed more money.

4. a. We painted our kitchen.
   b. We paint our kitchen.

5. a. The planes landed at the airport.
   b. The planes land at the airport.

6. a. We wait for the train.
   b. We waited for the train.

7. a. We planned meals.
   b. We plan meals.

8. a. We washed our car.
   b. We wash our car.

9. a. They looked at pictures.
   b. They look at pictures.

10. a. The children play at school.
    b. The children played at school.

6 Weak syllables
Linking vowels

Can I help you? Yes, I'd like a pizza.

A Vowels in strong and weak syllables

Strong	Regular	Weak
a	a	ə
e	e	ə
i	i	ə
o	o	ə
u	u	ə
Very easy to hear	Easy to hear	Hard to hear

B Rules for strong and weak syllables

1 Review these rules.

The Strong Syllable Rules

When you say a word alone:

1. Each word has one strong syllable.
2. The vowel in a strong syllable is long.

paper   pencil   computer

When you say words in a sentence:

3. One word is the most important.
4. The vowel in the strong syllable of the important word is extra long.

I need a pencil .   I needed a pencil.

Unit 6 • 35

6 Weak syllables
Linking vowels

Unit overview

This unit begins by focusing on the *schwa,* the weak, or de-stressed, vowel sound. Although there is no alphabet letter for it, it is the most common vowel sound in spoken English. This sound is relatively uncommon in world languages, so many students need practice hearing it. The focus on the schwa is intended mainly to aid listening comprehension. Incorporating the sound into their spoken English is often difficult for beginning learners.

The quality of the schwa sound is neutral, as in the first syllable of the word *about.* In fact, any vowel letter can be pronounced as schwa when it is in an unstressed syllable. (There are actually three different forms of weak vowels, but from a beginning student's point of view they all sound pretty much alike.)

After practice in recognizing and saying weak and strong syllables, learners listen to and practice vowel linking, as in *coffee and milk.* This leads to tasks in which students practice saying the commonly de-stressed words *and, of,* and *a.* Finally, students integrate the skills practiced in this unit in a restaurant conversation.

A Vowels in strong and weak syllables

The short, obscure vowel – or schwa – at the center of a weak (de-stressed) English syllable is perhaps the greatest barrier to learners' listening comprehension.

To introduce the concept of the weak syllable to students, call their attention to the illustrations in the box. The three figures in the box represent strong (stressed), regular, and weak (de-stressed) vowels.

B Rules for strong and weak syllables

Go over the rules on pages 35 and 36 with students. It may be useful to give students rubber bands to illustrate vowel length, as suggested in Unit 5.

Teaching Tip

Write these three example words on the board in big letters: *paper, Monday, pizza*. Underneath them write each word again, but rewriting the strong *a* in *paper* as a stretched *a* and the weak *a* in *pizza* as a schwa. Choose three students who like acting to play the parts of strong, regular, and weak vowels. Have them imitate the positions of the figures in the illustrations on page 35 and position them under the appropriate syllables. This activity is further developed on page T-45.

C Which vowel sounds are weak?

Tell students that in Unit 5 they listened for the strong syllable in some of these words, and now they are going to listen for the weak syllables. Have them look at the example done for them in item 1 before listening to the audio program, to be sure they understand what to do. After students listen, have them put the answers on the board and check as a class.

2 Read these new rules.

> **The Weak Syllable Rules**
>
> 1. The vowels in some syllables keep their regular sound. But some syllables get weak.
>
>
>
> 2. The vowels in weak syllables are short and not clear.
> 3. All weak vowels sound the same.
> 4. The weak vowel sound is the most common sound in spoken English.
>
> | paper | pencil | computer |
> |-------|--------|----------|
> | papər | pencəl | cəmputər |

3 Listen.

1. salad   saləd
2. lemon   lemən
3. vanilla   vənillə
4. sandwich   sandwəch
5. lemonade   lemənade
6. tomato   təmato

C Which vowel sounds are weak?

1 Listen. Draw a line through the weak vowels.

1. banana
2. Canada
3. freezer
4. blanket
5. vanilla
6. China
7. Japan

2 Check your answers with the class.

🎧 D *Saying strong and weak syllables*

Listen. Say each word two times.

Canada	America	Japan	China	Mexico
Canədə	əmerəcə	Jəpan	Chinə	Mexəco

🎧 E *Strong and weak syllables in food names*

Listen. Say each word two times. Remember to make the strong vowels long and the weak vowels short.

1. tomato
   təmato
2. burger
   burgər
3. sesame bun
   sesəme bun
4. ketchup
   ketchəp
5. soda
   sodə

6. pizza
   pizzə
7. spaghetti
   spəghetti
8. pepperoni
   peppəroni
9. vanilla
   vənillə
10. chocolate
    choclət

🎧 F *Linking vowels*

A vowel sound at the end of a word links to a vowel at the beginning of the next word.

Listen. Say each group of words two times.

1. coffee and milk   coffeeeand milk
2. tea and lemon   teaeeand lemon
3. pizza and salad   pizzaaaand salad
4. vanilla ice cream   vanillaaaice cream
5. banana or apple   bananaaaor apple

🎧 D *Saying strong and weak syllables*

Students may have very different pronunciations of (or even different words for) these country names in their own languages. As they listen to and repeat the names, students can practice with rubber bands or gestures to reinforce the pronunciations.

🎧 E *Strong and weak syllables in food names*

Have students listen to the audio program and repeat each word at least two times.

Note: The word *pizza* /'piːt•sə/ doesn't follow the One Vowel Rule because it is a word borrowed from a different language.

🎧 F *Linking vowels*

In earlier units, students practiced linking with *N* and *M*. Tell them that vowels can also link to each other.

Linking these vowels helps learners realize why these combinations of words in which the first word ends with a vowel and the second word begins with a vowel (e.g., *vanilla ice*) sound like one word /və,nɪl•ə 'ɑɪs/.

G Weak "and"

Tell students that it is not only syllables that can be weak – whole words can be weak too. After students listen to the audio program and repeat the phrases, encourage them to think of other examples with *and* that they may have heard, such as *fish 'n' chips, snow 'n' ice, dogs 'n' cats, hot 'n' cold, boys 'n' girls.*

H Weak "and," "of," and "a"

Have students listen to the phrases on the audio program and repeat them two times.

Note: Although *pizza* /'piːt•sə/ with its alphabet vowel sound I^y doesn't follow the vowel rules, the word *slice* does, as in:

a slice of pizza
a slice of cake
a slice of cheese

Soup /suːp/ also does not follow the vowel rules.

G Weak "and"

Usually the word "and" is so weak that it sounds like ən . Listen. Say each group of words two times.

1. coffee and cream
   coffee ən cream

2. tea and lemon
   tea ən lemən

3. coffee and cake
   coffee ən cake

4. burger and fries
   burgər ən fries

H Weak "and," "of," and "a"

Listen to the weak sounds of "and," "of," and "a." Say each group of words two times.

1. a cup of coffee
   ə cup ə coffee

2. a bowl of soup
   ə bowl ə soup

3. a slice of pie
   ə slice ə pie

4. a slice of lemon pie
   ə slice ə lemən pie

5. a burger with cheese, ketchup, and fries
   ə burgər with cheese, ketchəp, ən fries

6. a pizza with cheese and tomatoes
   ə pizzə with cheese ən təmatoes

7. a burger and tomato soup
   ə burgər ən təmatə soup

I Review: The One Vowel Rule

1 Review this rule.

The One Vowel Rule

When there is only one vowel letter in a syllable:

    1. The vowel letter does NOT say its alphabet name.
    2. The vowel letter says its RELATIVE sound.

This rule is true for many words.

can	pencil	finger	hot	summer
Mack	Jenny	Kitty	John	Russ

---

2 Listen. Say each word two times.

A	E	I	O	U
salad	lemon	milk	chocolate	bun
banana	egg	vanilla	bottle	butter
sandwich	ketchup	chicken	clock	mustard

J Music of English ♪♪♪

Listen. Say each sentence two times.

Cən I help you?

Yes. I'd like ə pīzzə.

What sīze?

Eləphənt-size!

I Review: The One Vowel Rule

Review the One Vowel Rule with students. Before they listen to the audio program, remind them to notice the weak sounds.

J Music of English

The exclamation point can give students a chance to express enthusiasm, by using their hands to show how big an elephant-size pizza would be. The hand gesture should occur at the first syllable of *elephant* so that the physical display matches the intonational emphasis.

Gestures are culturally fixed and may be transferred into a second language. On the other hand, when learners are feeling tense in a new language, they often speak in a monotone and without any physical movement. In English, gestures need to co-occur with spoken emphasis, in order to make that emphasis quite clear. This can be demonstrated by showing a brief section of a video of a TV comedy or a speech. The same short section should be shown several times, both with and without sound so that students can see how gesture is systematically matched with speech. One way to describe this is that "the dance always goes with the music."

Students can be helped to mark the important emphasis points by practicing some kind of gesture with their hands, or some facial gesture, such as eyebrow raising. This may seem funny at first, especially for students coming from cultures that tend to use only very subtle facial gestures to show emphasis or opinion.

For students from such a background, it may be important to point out that gesture is not only used to make the emphasis clear to the listener, but also to show that a listener is actually listening. Usually there will be a nod, raising of eyebrows, some little noise, or some other response to show attentiveness, if not actual agreement. A face that shows no response to what the other person is saying usually signals disagreement or perhaps even anger. This physical responsiveness is another point students can watch for in a silent section of video.

Note: After students listen to the audio program and repeat the sentences, have them repeat the exchange at least once more as a whole piece, to show how the meanings and intonation patterns of the sentences are linked.

K The Elephant Eatery

Have students look at the menu while they listen to the audio program and repeat the words. When they finish, you can ask them if they have tried any of the foods listed on the menu. You can also ask them what items on the menu sound good or strange to them.

Note: Iced tea is pronounced the same as *ice tea* /aɪsˈtiː/ and is sometimes spelled that way on menus.

Artichokes /ˈɑrt̬•əˌtʃoʊks/ is not a common word, but was chosen to show students that they can now figure out the pronunciation of an unfamiliar word syllable by syllable. There is a drawing of an artichoke on the menu. It is a green vegetable composed of hard leaves with a sharp thorn at the tip of each leaf and a soft edible part at the base. The heart of the artichoke is popular in salads and sometimes as a topping for pizza.

L Pair work: In the Elephant Eatery

Have students listen to the conversation on the audio program and then practice it with a partner. Encourage them to over-act and use gestures. Choose one or two pairs to perform the conversation for the class.

K The Elephant Eatery

Look at the menu. Listen. Say each food two times.

THE ELEPHANT EATERY
Elephant-Size Pizza

SOUP (cup or bowl)
Tomato Soup, Potato Soup

SALAD
Green Salad
Carrot and Raisin Salad

PIZZA
Small   12 inches
Medium   14 inches
Elephant-size 16 inches

EXTRA TOPPINGS
Extra cheese, tomatoes, pepperoni, onions, artichokes

BEVERAGES
Coffee, tea, iced tea, soda, lemonade

L Pair work: In the Elephant Eatery

1 Listen to the conversation.

2 Say the conversation with a partner. Take turns as the server and the customer.

Server: Can I help you?
Customer: Yes, I'd like a pizza and coffee.
Server: What kind of pizza? Plain, cheese, or with everything?
Customer: What's everything?
Server: Cheese, tomatoes, onions, pepperoni, and artichokes.
Customer: Great! I want one with everything!
Server: What size?
Customer: Elephant-size! I'm very hungry!

40 • Unit 6

M Pair work: Ordering food

Order food from the Elephant Eatery menu. Take turns as the server and the customer.

Example

> Server: Can I help you?
> Customer: Yes, I'd like a pizza with pepperoni.
> Server: What size?
> Customer: Medium.
> Server: Okay. Anything else?
> Customer: A cup of coffee, please.
> Server: Coming right up!

N Food game   EXTRA

1 Divide into teams.

2 Write food words with your team.

3 Circle the strong syllable in each word.

4 After five minutes, compare your words. Each team gets one point for each correct answer.

Examples

Students may think of foods in which both syllables have roughly equal strength and so are worth two points for the circled syllables (e.g., *beefsteak, pancakes, meatloaf*). Other foods to suggest if they get stuck:

(tu)na
(ap)ples
(pea)ches
(mus)tard
(vin)egar
(cook)ies
(pu)dding
(mu)ffin
(le)ttuce
(cra)ckers
(om)elet
as(par)agus
spa(ghe)tti

See Unit 6 Quiz on page T-136.

M Pair work: Ordering food

Encourage students to use gestures as they did in L. If they are able, students can add menu items to make this role play more fun (*spaghetti, steak, fruit salad,* etc.). When they finish, choose one or two pairs to perform their conversations for the class.

N Food game   EXTRA

Put students into groups of four or five and have them make a list of food words. The food names should have two or more syllables. Make the game more interesting by awarding points separately for correctly identifying the number of syllables and for circling the strong syllable.

7 The most important word

Unit overview

In Unit 7, students build on what they learned about strong and weak syllables by focusing on word emphasis in sentences. In English, emphasis is mainly signaled by intonation with a large pitch change on the most important word. Other languages use different means to make clear which word is most important: perhaps word order, or a special particle or word that alerts the listener to notice a certain part of a message. Language-specific systems for emphasis are learned so early that they are applied unconsciously to any new language, so it is necessary to train students to notice the length difference and the change of pitch on the primary stress (strong syllable) of the most important word.

In this unit, students practice specific communication skills connected with word emphasis: pointing out and clarifying misunderstandings, and correcting mistakes about the date and time.

---

7 The most important word

Are you going to eat supper at nine?
No, at six.

A The most important thing

Look at these pictures. What makes the rabbit easy to see?

Hard to see

Easy to see

> **Easy to see**
> The rabbit is easy to see when:
> • it jumps up
> • it is extra long
> • the rabbit is light, and the leaves are dark

B The most important word

1 What makes a word easy to hear?

> **Easy to hear**
> In English, a word is easy to hear when:
> • the strong syllable jumps up or down
> • the vowel in the strong syllable is extra long
> • the other words in the sentence are weak

A The most important thing

Call students' attention to the two pictures of the rabbit, and ask *What makes the rabbit easy to see?* If students need help, the answer to this question is in the box just beneath the pictures. These graphic images are meant to convey the importance of intonation.

B The most important word

1. The box labeled *Easy to hear* is meant to teach students that the pitch change, the lengthening of the primary stress, and the weakening of many of the vowels are mechanisms to highlight the focus of a sentence or thought group. Linking ties the words in a thought group together, making a rhythmic context in which the focus word can easily be identified by the listener. In fact, there is often little real lengthening for the stressed syllable of any word unless it is the focus of a thought group. For that reason, from this point onward in the book, only the primary stress of the focus word will be practiced.

2 Listen.

A: What's the matter?

 What's the m**a**tter?

B: I lost a ticket.

I lost a t**i**cket.

A: What's it for?

What's it f**or**?

B: It's for a show.

It's for a sh**ow**.

3 Read these rules.

> *Rules for the Most Important Word*
>
> 1. Each sentence has one most important word.
>
>   What's the **matter**?
>
> 2. The vowel sound in the strong syllable of that word is extra long.
>
>   What's the m**a**tter?
>
> 3. The voice goes up or down on the strong syllable in the most important word.
>
>   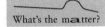 What's the m**a**tter?   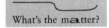 What's the m**a**tter?

 C *Music of English* ♩♪

Listen. Say these sentences two times.

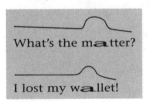

What's the m**a**tter?

I lost my w**a**llet!

Unit 7 • **43**

---

2. Play the audio program and encourage students to trace the pitch lines in the Student's Book as they listen to help them feel how the pitch changes on the focus word in each sentence.

3. Go over the rules for the most important word. In some languages, the most important word is automatically placed at a particular position in the sentence. But since this word can be anywhere in an English sentence, the intonational marking is crucial.

It is not so important in which direction the voice changes pitch. What really matters is that there is a change either up or down from the baseline pitch. This calls the listener's attention to the focus word. Students often go up or down on many words, hoping this will make them more intelligible. But this is as damaging to the English system of intonational marking as is the other common way of speaking a new language – in a monotone. English has very little syntactic or other means to call attention to the crucial word, so the pitch change is an essential signal of importance/focus.

Note: If a word is said alone, it is a complete utterance and therefore the word will have the lengthening and pitch change of a thought group. That means that *electrification* will have the same musical pattern as *We went to the station.*

🎧 **C** *Music of English*

To introduce this task, show students your wallet and ask *What's this called?* When they answer, ask *What's it for?* Then play the audio program and have students repeat the sentences.

Note: After students listen to the audio program and repeat the sentences, have them repeat the exchange at least once more as a whole piece, to show how the meanings and intonation patterns of the sentences are linked.

💡 *Teaching Tip*

A kazoo (a toy humming instrument) is an excellent tool for helping students pay attention to the change of pitch. The kazoo amplifies the vibration in the vocal cords and thus conveys the pitch pattern of the voice without the distraction of individual sounds. You may be able to buy kazoos at a party supply store, but if they are not available where you live, you can simply "sing" the pitch pattern with an "ahhhh" sound. Students should practice this in chorus, until all the group is singing the melody of the sentence together accurately. Then they will be ready to do it with the words.

Using your finger to draw the pattern in the air while saying the sentence can give a visual signal to the students. If they do it themselves, this makes their practice more kinesthetic.

Do not rush this kind of practice. If it is done thoroughly, it can give students confidence in marrying the music to the words.

D *Pair work: The most important word*

Before students say the conversations, play the audio program so they can hear the correct intonation.

E *Pair work: Finding the most important word*

Now students must decide which word is most important. They should follow the model in task D. If students have enough vocabulary, they can supply words of their own to these dialogues about losing things. Choose one or two pairs to perform their conversations for the class.

D *Pair work: The most important word*

1 Listen to the conversations.

2 Say these conversations two times with a partner. Go up or down on the most important word.

1. The Glasses

   Sue: What's the `matter`? ("Matter" is the important word.)

   Ted: I lost my `glasses`. ("Glasses" is the important word.)

   Sue: What `kind` of glasses? ("Kind" is the important word.)

   Ted: `Reading` glasses. ("Reading" is the important word.)

2. The Keys

   Mike: What's the `matter`? ("Matter" is the important word.)

   Jane: I lost my `keys`. ("Keys" is the important word.)

   Mike: `Which` keys? ("Which" is the important word.)

   Jane: My `car` keys. ("Car" is the important word.)

E *Pair work: Finding the most important word*

1 Circle the most important word in each sentence.

2 Say these conversations two times with a partner.

1. The Shoes
   Jean : What's (wrong)?
   Joan : I lost my (shoes.)
   Jean : (Which) shoes?
   Joan : My (tennis) shoes.

2. The Dog
   Jim: What's the problem?
   Mike: I lost my dog.
   Jim: What kind of dog?
   Mike: A brown dog. A small brown dog.
   Jim: I saw a small brown dog. It was at the supermarket.

3. A Letter
   Bob: What are you doing?
   Jenny: I'm writing a letter.
   Bob: What kind of letter?
   Jenny: A business letter.
   Bob: What kind of business?
   Jenny: Personal business!

F ***Music of English*** ♫♪

Listen. Say each sentence two times.

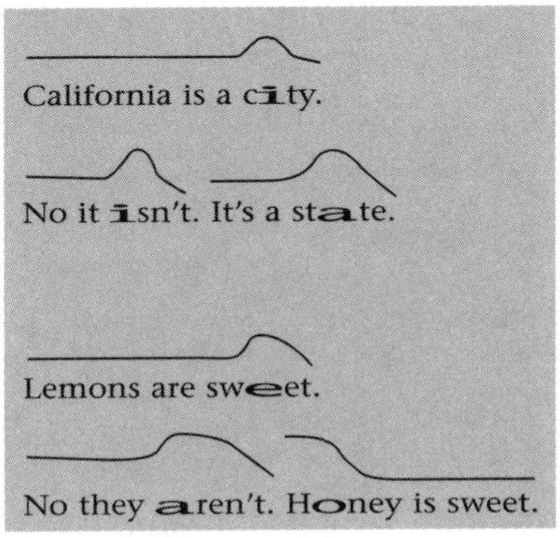
California is a city.
No it isn't. It's a state.
Lemons are sweet.
No they aren't. Honey is sweet.

F Music of English

This "music box" introduces the useful skill of polite disagreement. It also gives students an opportunity to work on word order and the plural/singular distinction for auxiliary verbs in short answers.

Note: Although usually a sentence such as *No it isn't.* is written with a comma after *No,* the comma is omitted here in order to make the pitch pattern easier for students to practice. On page 48, the comma is added. This makes two thought groups, so the intonation is a bit more complicated.

Teaching Tip

A challenging and entertaining way to encourage a physical sense of the music in these sentences is through the game of "Syllablettes," developed by William Acton. In this game, teams plan how to demonstrate a sentence, building on the practice suggested in the beginning of Unit 6 (see page T-36). Each student represents one syllable and must show their forms as strong, regular, or weak. Adventurous teams could add in linking. Then they should practice saying their syllables in sequence while physically demonstrating the degree of syllable strength, producing the sentence in a smooth, continuous flow.

G Pair work: Disagreement

You can introduce this task by making some obviously incorrect statements to the class.

Examples

> This is a Spanish class.
>
> Today is very hot/cold. (Say the opposite of the truth.)
>
> This is a dog. (Hold up a textbook.)

Students may be surprised by this at first, but you can shake your head no, and encourage them to disagree with you. Then have students circle the most important word in each sentence, and say the conversations two times with a partner. They should switch roles the second time.

Because it is important for students to recognize which is the crucial word in the disagreements, this exercise should be practiced several times. To make it more interesting and useful, have students practice with different partners.

G Pair work: Disagreement

1 Circle the most important word in each sentence.

2 Say these conversations two times with a partner. Go up or down on the strong syllable in the important word.

1. A: California is a (city).
   B: No it isn't. It's a (state).

2. A: Ice is hot.
   B: No it isn't. It's cold.

3. A: Lemons are sweet.
   B: No they aren't. Honey is sweet.

4. A: Babies are bigger than children.
   B: No they aren't. They're smaller than children.

5. A: Fish eat grass.
   B: No they don't. They eat smaller fish.

6. A: The world is flat.
   B: No it isn't. It's round.

7. A: You buy books at a library.
   B: No you don't. You buy books at a bookstore.

8. A: You borrow books at a bookstore.
   B: No you don't. You borrow books at a library.

9. A: Cars travel in the air.
   B: No they don't. They travel on the road.

10. A: Toronto is the capital of Canada.
    B: No it isn't. Ottawa is the capital of Canada.

Unit 7

🎧 H Music of English 🎵

Listen. Say each sentence two times.

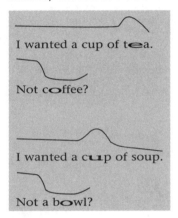

I wanted a cup of tea.

Not coffee?

I wanted a cup of soup.

Not a bowl?

I Pair work: Misunderstandings

1 Customer, say **a** or **b**.

2 Server, answer.

3 Take turns as the customer and server.

Examples

Customer:	I wanted **two** lemonades.
Server:	Not one?
Customer:	I wanted a cup of **soup**.
Server:	Not coffee?

Customer	Server
1. a. I wanted a cup of **soup**.	Not coffee?
b. I wanted a **cup** of soup.	Not a bowl?
2. a. I wanted **two** lemonades.	Not one?
b. I wanted two **lemonades**.	Not Cokes?

Unit 7 • **47**

🎧 H Music of English

In certain cultures, people will not usually point out misunderstandings if they are served the wrong thing at a restaurant. Tell students that in most English-speaking cultures it is all right to do so. This exercise will give them the intonation to point out misunderstandings clearly and politely.

I Pair work: Misunderstandings

After reading the directions, model the task by taking the part of Student A and choosing someone in the class to take the part of Student B. Then put students into pairs and have them take turns correcting and responding to the misunderstandings. Remind students to choose **a** or **b** at random, to keep the exercise interesting. If students have enough vocabulary, they can develop some of their own misunderstandings, and then share them with the class.

Note: After students listen to the audio program and repeat the sentences, have them repeat the two exchanges at least once more as whole pieces, to show how the meanings and intonation patterns of the sentences are linked.

T-47

Note: In the answer to **6a**, *Oh, I thought you wanted a small glass, wanted* is emphasized because this is exactly what the server thought.

J *Music of English*

Play the audio program for students and have them repeat the sentences at least two times. You could demonstrate how exaggerating the intonation even more makes the questioner sound surprised or shocked.

Note: After students listen to the audio program and repeat the sentences, have them repeat the two exchanges at least once more as whole pieces, to show how the meanings and intonation patterns of the sentences are linked.

3. a. But I wanted lemon **pie**!   Not ice cream?
   b. But I wanted **lemon** pie!   Not apple?

4. a. I asked for potato **salad**.   Not soup?
   b. I asked for **potato** salad.   Not tomato?

5. a. This is a tuna **sandwich**!   Oh, did you want tuna salad?
   b. This is a **tuna** sandwich!   Oh, did you want egg?

6. a. That's a **small** glass!   Oh, I thought you wanted a small glass.
   b. That's a small **glass**!   Oh, did you want a cup?

J *Music of English* 🎵♪

Listen. Say each sentence two times.

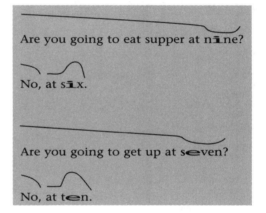

Are you going to eat supper at n**ī**ne?

No, at s**ī**x.

Are you going to get up at s**e**ven?

No, at t**e**n.

K Pair work: Correcting a mistake about time

1 Student A, ask a question about an activity from the Activities box below. Use any time of day.

2 Student B, say "No" and give another time.

3 Take turns asking questions. Remember to go up or down on the important word.

Examples

> Student A: Are you going to get up at seven?
> Student B: No, at **nine**.
>
> Student B: Are you going to meet a friend at one?
> Student A: No, at **two**.

Activities

eat breakfast	get up	catch a bus
eat lunch	go to work	meet a friend
eat supper	have a snack	go to bed

L Review: Counting syllables ☐☐☐

1 Listen. Write the number of syllables.

1. Monday _2_
2. Tuesday _2_
3. Wednesday _2_
4. Thursday _2_
5. Friday _2_
6. Saturday _3_
7. Sunday _2_

2 Check your answers with the class.

K Pair work: Correcting a mistake about time

In this exercise, students practice a useful social skill: correcting mistakes or misunderstandings about time. This will be especially helpful when they need to make appointments or reservations in English.

Read the instructions aloud and go over the examples in the box with the students. Circulate around the room to check on students' work as they do the exercise to make sure they go up or down on the most important word.

L Review: Counting syllables

After students listen to the days of the week and write the number of syllables, have them practice saying the days aloud. This will prepare them for the next task, in which they correct mistakes about the days of the week.

Pair work: Correcting a mistake about the day

This exercise is similar to K, but students correct information about days rather than times. Note that the sentences in this unit are longer and the grammar is more complicated than in previous units. The length of the sentence, *Are you going to see the doctor on Monday?*, makes it harder for the student to decide which part of the sentence is most important to highlight it.

 Teaching Tip

If students have enough language, this can be made into an information gap exercise. Make copies of a blank page of a weekly appointment book for students. Put students into pairs, and have partners ask each other if they plan to do something at a particular hour or day of the week and fill in each other's schedules. The important thing to practice is emphasizing the important information and correcting misinformation. When the speaker successfully emphasizes a particular word (the hour or the day of the week), it is like shining a flashlight beam on the exact information desired.

See Unit 7 Quiz on page T-137.

M **Pair work: Correcting a mistake about the day**

1 Student A, ask a question about an activity from the Activities box. Choose any day.

2 Student B, say "No" and give another day.

3 Take turns asking questions.

Examples

> Student A: Are you going to see the doctor on Monday?
> Student B: No, **Friday**.
>
> Student B: Are you going to play soccer on Thursday?
> Student A: No, **Saturday**.

Activities

see the doctor	study English	play soccer
visit friends	go to class	wash your car
bake a cake	shop for clothes	buy a car
fly to New York	write a letter	wash the dog

Days

Monday	Friday
Tuesday	Saturday
Wednesday	Sunday
Thursday	

8 Stop sound T/D and continuing sound S/Z
Linking with T/D and S/Z

How do you spell "cakes"?
Is she running? No, she's reading.

 A _Stop sounds and continuing sounds_

1 Look at these pictures.

Stop sound T/D   Continuing sound S/Z

Looking to the front

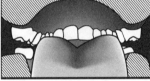

Looking down

 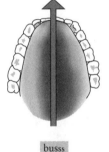

but   busss

STOP   →

Air stops   Air continues

Unit 8 • **51**

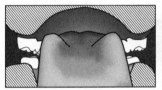 **8 Stop sound T/D and continuing sound S/Z Linking with T/D and S/Z**

Unit overview

Unit 8 introduces the contrasting concepts of stop sounds and continuing sounds (or *continuants*), using the pairs T and D (/t/, /d/) and S and Z (/s/, /z/). The final sounds S and Z are particularly important in English because they mark plural nouns, third-person singular verbs, and possessives.

The continuing sounds S and Z are distinguished only by the presence or absence of vibration, or *voicing*, in the vocal cords. That is, the final sound in *bus* /s/ is unvoiced, and the final sound in *buzz* /z/ is voiced. The same is true for T and D: They are alike in every way except for voicing. The voiced/unvoiced distinction is not crucial for students at this stage of learning. It is not presented in the Student's Book, in an effort to keep things simple and to allow students to concentrate on the stop/continuing sound distinction. Accordingly, the two stop sounds T and D are represented throughout the book as one sound, T/D, and S and Z are represented as S/Z.

 A _Stop sounds and continuing sounds_

1. Call students' attention to the diagrams on this page. Unlike traditional side view drawings, these illustrations aim to show how changes in the way the air flows through the mouth create stops and continuing sounds. To make the stop sound T/D, the tongue blocks airflow out of the mouth by pressing against the tooth ridge all the way around the front of the mouth. To make the continuing sound S/Z, air is forced through a narrow V-shaped passage at high pressure. The friction (or *turbulence*) created by the flow of air through this narrow passage is the cause of the characteristic hissing associated with sibilant sounds. It also is what distinguishes these sounds from TH and T/D, which will be introduced in Unit 15.

To demonstrate the difference between a stop and a continuing sound, walk around the room saying *bus,* continuing the S until you run out of air. Then say *but,* throwing up the palm of your hand facing the class, in a "stop" gesture, at the

T-51

end of the word. Don't release any air after the *T* sound; just stop. Another approach is to move your hand across the space in front of you to represent a continuing sound as you say *bus*, and then make the stop gesture with the hand when you say *but*. These signals can be used by students also, to help them concentrate on the stop/continuing sound distinction, and they match nicely the stop sign and arrow.

The difference between a stop and a continuing sound is most apparent at the end of a word, and therefore that is the position where it is easiest to demonstrate. However, a more important reason to concentrate only on the ends of words is that this is where stops and continuing sounds can function as grammatical signals, for example: *book / books, can / can't, I go / I'd go.*

Allow students to try out the feel of these sounds for themselves quietly while they look at the mouth pictures. Time given to this physical introspection and experimentation is not the same as asking students to listen and repeat words. It gives students a personal orientation to the airflow requirements of the two sounds. However, in the next few tasks, students should *not* repeat the words they hear, but concentrate only on listening.

Note: The stop sounds in English are *P* /p/, *B* /b/, *T* /t/, *D* /d/, *K* /k/, and *G* /g/ plus the "combination sounds" (*affricates*) *CH* /tʃ/ as in *church* and *J* /dʒ/ as in *judge*. All the other sounds, including vowels, are continuants.

---

2 Listen for the sound at the end of each word. Do not say the words.

STOP →

	STOP	→
1.	but	bus
	but	busss
2.	boat	boats
	boat	boatsss
3.	had	has
	had	hazzz
4.	seat	seats
	seat	seatsss
5.	it	is
	it	izzz
6.	hit	his
	hit	hizzz
7.	coat	coats
	coat	coatsss

B Which word is different?

1 Listen. Mark the different word.

	X	Y	Z	
1.			✔	(right, right, rice)
2.			✓	
3.	✓			
4.	✓			
5.			✓	
6.		✓		
7.		✓		
8.			✓	

2 Listen again.

---

2. In this exercise, students just listen and should not try to repeat the words. Repeating what they have just heard will tend to obscure the acoustic imprint in their minds. It is better that they be encouraged to be patient and just listen at this stage.

Teaching Tip

Use a fluffy feather, strip of tissue paper, or lighted candle to demonstrate the difference between a stop (no airflow) and a continuant. Hold the object close to the lips, and the airflow of a continuing sound will make it flutter.

C Which word do you hear?

1 Listen. Circle the word you hear.

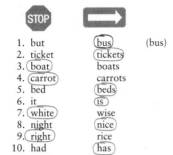

	STOP	
1.	but	(bus) (bus)
2.	ticket	(tickets)
3.	(boat)	boats
4.	(carrot)	carrots
5.	bed	(beds)
6.	it	(is)
7.	(white)	wise
8.	night	(nice)
9.	(right)	rice
10.	had	(has)

2 Listen again.

D Final sounds: Stop or continue?

1 Cover the words.

2 Listen to each word. Mark if the final sound stops or continues.

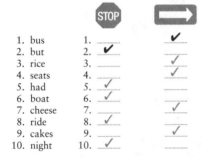

		STOP		
1.	bus	1.	✔
2.	but	2. ✔	
3.	rice	3.	✓
4.	seats	4.	✓
5.	had	5. ✓	
6.	boat	6. ✓	
7.	cheese	7.	✓
8.	ride	8. ✓	
9.	cakes	9.	✓
10.	night	10. ✓	

3 Look at the words. Listen again.

Unit 8 • 53

B Which word is different?

Have students listen and check the different word. Do not worry about the difference between *D* and *T* or *S* and *Z*. Only ask students to notice whether the final sound is a stop or a continuing sound.

Write the answers on the board or have the students say the letters of the correct answers in unison.

Audio script

1. right, right, rice
   /raɪt/, /raɪt/, /raɪs/

2. bus, bus, but
   /bʌs/, /bʌs/, /bʌt/

3. white, wise, wise
   /waɪt/, /waɪz/, /waɪz/

4. beds, bed, bed
   /bedz/, /bed/, /bed/

5. night, night, nice
   /naɪt/, /naɪt/, /naɪs/

6. boat, boats, boat
   /boʊt/, /boʊts/, /boʊt/

7. flight, flies, flight
   /flaɪt/, /flaɪz/, /flaɪt/

8. hat, hat, hats
   /hæt/, /hæt/, /hæts/

C Which word do you hear?

Have students circle the words they hear. When checking answers, you might want to have students tell you whether the final sounds stop or continue.

Audio script

1.	bus	/bʌs/
2.	tickets	/ˈtɪk•əts/
3.	boat	/boʊt/
4.	carrot	/ˈkær•ət/
5.	beds	/bedz/
6.	is	/ɪz/
7.	white	/waɪt/
8.	nice	/naɪs/
9.	right	/raɪt/
10.	has	/hæz/

D Final sounds: Stop or continue?

Make sure students cover the words the first time they listen to this exercise. They should be relying on their ears rather than on the spelling.

E Pair work: Is it one or more than one?

Go over the instructions and examples with your students. It can be useful to give some additional examples and have students respond in unison before they begin the pair work. Remind them to choose **a** or **b** words at random to keep the activity challenging. Depending on the level of the class, it may be appropriate to teach students the words *singular* and *plural*.

If possible, have students change partners two or three times. If students all belong to the same first language group, this kind of pair work may not work as well as in a multilingual class because the students may use non-English cues to signal a difficult sound (e.g., extra tension in their voice or body for the sound students know is extra difficult). Even in this situation, the practice is useful because it helps focus on the final consonant and the fact that it makes a difference to meaning.

F Music of English

It may help students to hum these questions first, or use a kazoo. Another way to help produce the proper emphasis is to have students "draw" the melody in the air with a hand. Many other kinds of active responses can also be used: Have students rise up a bit from their seats as they emphasize the important syllable, or raise their eyebrows, or bow a bit from the waist. Physical marking of the important syllable can bring major improvement in intelligibility, because musical emphasis of this syllable is probably the single most important key to communication in spoken English.

E Pair work: Is it one or more than one?

1 Student A, say word **a** or **b**.

2 Student B, if you hear a word meaning one thing, hold up one finger. If you hear a word meaning more than one thing, hold up all five fingers.

3 Take turns saying words.

Examples

> Student A: Carrots.
> Student B: (Hold up all five fingers.)
>
> Student B: Jacket.
> Student A: (Hold up one finger.)

1. a. carrot
    b. carrots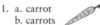

2. a. jackets
    b. jacket

3. a. fruit
    b. fruits

4. a. postcard
    b. postcards

5. a. coats
    b. coat

6. a. lemonade
    b. lemonades

7. a. ticket
    b. tickets

8. a. shake
    b. shakes

9. a. Coke
    b. Cokes

10. a. seat
    b. seats

F Music of English ♫♪

Listen. Say each sentence two times.

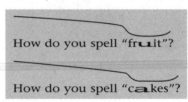

How do you spell "fruit"?

How do you spell "cakes"?

G ***Pair work: How do you spell "hats"?***

1 Student A, ask question **a** or **b**.

2 Student B, spell the word.

3 Student A, if the spelling is correct, say "Right." If it is wrong, say the word again.

4 Take turns asking questions.

Examples

> Student A: How do you spell "hats"?
> Student B: H - A - T - S.
> Student A: Right.
>
> Student B: How do you spell "beds"?
> Student A: B - E - D.
> Student B: No, "beds."
> Student A: B - E - D - S.

1. a. How do you spell "hat"?   H - A - T.
   b. How do you spell "hats"?   H - A - T - S.

2. a. How do you spell "beds"?   B - E - D - S.
   b. How do you spell "bed"?   B - E - D.

3. a. How do you spell "fruit"?   F - R - U - I - T.
   b. How do you spell "fruits"?   F - R - U - I - T - S.

4. a. How do you spell "white"?   W - H - I - T - E.
   b. How do you spell "wise"?   W - I - S - E.

5. a. How do you spell "suit"?   S - U - I - T.
   b. How do you spell "suits"?   S - U - I - T - S.

6. a. How do you spell "plate"?   P - L - A - T - E.
   b. How do you spell "plays"?   P - L - A - Y - S.

7. a. How do you spell "right"?   R - I - G - H - T.
   b. How do you spell "rice"?   R - I - C - E.

8. a. How do you spell "repeat"?   R - E - P - E - A -T.
   b. How do you spell "repeats"?   R - E - P - E - A - T - S.

Unit 8 • 55

G ***Pair work: How do you spell "hats"?***

After reading the directions, ask students to read the examples. Then model the task by taking the part of Student A and choosing someone in the class to take the part of Student B. Act out choosing a question to ask, then have Student B answer your question. Confirm or correct the answer. Then put students into pairs. You could give the class a couple of additional examples and have them answer in unison before they start the pair work.

Note: Repeats (in item **8**) is more likely to be used as a third-person singular verb rather than a plural noun. This grammatical construction is harder to learn than the plural and is introduced here only so that students become used to hearing the sound of a final *S*.

When they study the third-person singular, this familiarity with the sound will help.

💡 ***Teaching Tip***

To help students say the cluster $D/T + S$, have them practice linking these phrases:

had six
white socks

H Linking with T/D

Students may be puzzled by the way *T*/*D* is referred to as one sound. Assure them that the tongue is in the same position for both sounds. The only difference is in the presence or absence of voicing, which means the vibration of the vocal cords. Students should not have to worry about voicing at this stage, because it is more important for them to get a firm grasp of the stop/continuant distinction.

Teaching Tip

Linking exercises can be done with the whole class or in pairs. Students may be helped to focus on this link by bringing their hands together or making linking "rings" out of thumbs and forefingers as they say the linking sound. Some people find this helps them concentrate, while others find it distracting. Give students an opportunity to experiment.

I Linking with S/Z

Go over the instructions with students before they listen to the audio program. Examples of *S*/*Z* linking to another continuing sound, rather than simply to a vowel, occur in sentences **2** (*Gus said*), **6** (*It's so*), **8** (*is new*), and **10** (*His mother*). If students are advanced enough, have them find these examples for you.

H Linking with T/D

T/D is a stop sound. It links to a vowel at the beginning of the next word.

1 Listen.

bad apples	badapples
Great idea!	Greatidea !
Find it.	Findit .

2 Listen. Say each sentence two times.

1. These are bad apples. These are badapples .
2. That's a great idea. That's a greatidea .
3. Please find it. Please findit .
4. This food is hot. This foodis hot.
5. They counted all the money. They countedall the money.
6. That blanket is clean. That blanketis clean.
7. We tried every key. We triedevery key.
8. That cat eats cheese. That cateats cheese.

I Linking with S/Z

S/Z is a continuing sound. A continuing sound links to a vowel sound at the beginning of the next word. It also links to other continuing sounds.

1 Listen.

Ann's address	Annzzzaddress
Gus said.	Gusssaid .
This is Ann.	ThisssizzzAnn .

2 Listen. Say each group of words two times.

1. They ordered cakes and coffee. They ordered cakesssand coffee.
2. Gus said, "Hello!" Gusssaid , "Hello!"
3. The books are on the shelf. The booksssare on the shelf.

4. Put the plates on the table.   Put the `platesson` the table.

5. I have tickets in my pocket.   I have `ticketsssin` my pocket.

6. It's so big!   `Itsssso` big!

7. It's stuff for the house.   `Itsssstuff` for the house.

8. Ann's address is new.   `Annzzzaddresssssizzznew` .

9. She's never here.   `Shezzznever` here.

10. His mother's always late.   `Hizzzmotherzzzalways` late.

🎧 **J** ___*Review: The Two Vowel Rule*___

> **The Two Vowel Rule**
>
> When there are two vowel letters in a syllable:
>
> 1. The first vowel says its alphabet name.
> 2. The second vowel is silent.
>
> cake   tea   ice   cone   cube

1 These words have two vowel letters together. Listen and say each word two times.

Aʸ	Eʸ	Iʸ	Oʷ	Uʷ
paid	reach	fries	boat	blue
train	need	cries	soak	fruit
plain	easy	tried	throat	true
explain	freezer	pies	coach	cue
remain	reason	applied	toe	barbecue
complain	reading	replied	loan	suitcase

2 These words have a silent letter -e at the end. Listen and say each word two times.

Aʸ	Eʸ	Iʸ	Oʷ	Uʷ
plane	these	price	note	cute
change	complete	retire	clothes	reduce
arrange	extreme	arrive	those	excuse
erase	Chinese	advice	telephone	refuse

🎧 **J** ___*Review: The Two Vowel Rule*___

Review the rule in the box with students. On the audio program, the students will hear the words read downward, in columns. If you feel they need more of a challenge, have them say the words across, in rows.

K *Music of English*

Students often emphasize a pronoun, even when that is not the main point. This may be because of a rule in their own language, but it is likely to confuse an English-speaking listener, since pronouns are emphasized in English only when they are specifically meant to be the focus of attention.

Note: After students listen to the audio program and repeat the sentences, have them repeat the two exchanges at least once more as whole pieces, to show how the meanings and intonation patterns of the sentences are linked.

L *Pair work: Correcting a mistake*

In this exercise, students review what they learned in Unit 7 about how to correct mistakes. Have students listen to and repeat the names of the activities in step 1. A useful approach is to point to or have students point to the pictures of activities in the box on page 59 as they listen. Then go over the instructions and examples with students before having them do the pair work. If they have enough language, they can ask questions about activities other than those listed in step 1.

K Music of English

Listen. Say each sentence two times.

Is she running?

No, she's reading.

Is he playing tennis?

Yes, he is.

L Pair work: Correcting a mistake

1 Listen. Say the names of these activities.

running	drinking water
sleeping	playing tennis
reading	playing soccer
eating	playing basketball

2 Student A, point to a picture in the Activities box on the next page. Ask a question about the picture.

3 Student B, answer.

4 Take turns asking questions.

Examples

Student A: Is she drinking water?
Student B: Yes, she is. (or No, she's **eating**.)

Student B: Is she playing basketball?
Student A: Yes, she is. (or No, she's playing **tennis**.)

Activities

M *S-Ball game* EXTRA

1 Divide into groups of four or five. Each group has a small ball. One student is the leader.

2 Leader, ask a question and then throw the ball to a student.

3 Student, catch the ball and answer the question. If you answer correctly (with a final **S** sound in the verb), you become the new leader.

Examples

> Leader: What does "writer" mean?
> (Throw the ball to a student.)
> Student A: A person who writes.
> (Student A becomes the leader.)
>
> Leader: What does "baker" mean?
> (Throw the ball to a student.)
> Student B: A person who bake.
> Leader: No. What does "baker" mean?
> (Throw the ball to a different student.)
> Student C: A person who bakes.

1. What does "writer" mean?
2. What does "baker" mean?
3. What does "worker" mean?
4. What does "reader" mean?
5. What does "cleaner" mean?
6. What does "leader" mean?
7. What does "speaker" mean?
8. What does "player" mean?
9. What does "painter" mean?
10. What does "trainer" mean?

Unit 8 • **59**

M *S-Ball game* EXTRA

To play this game, you will need to bring to class several small, lightweight balls – one for each group of four or five students. If no balls are readily available, you can have students crumple a sheet of paper into a ball. After reading the instructions, model the examples in the box with three students. Then put students into groups of four or five and have them play the game.

Don't let the Leader ask these questions in sequence (1, 2, 3, etc.) because that makes the game too easy. Accept either an *S* or a *Z* sound for all these word endings. Leave the voicing distinction for later teaching. The faster the game, the more fun, assuming the class is advanced enough to take the pressure.

See Unit 8 Quiz on page T-138.

9 Final sounds D and L Linking with L

Unit overview

Like Unit 8, this unit focuses on the distinction between word-final stops and continuants, this time with *D* /d/ and *L* /l/. This leads to tasks in which students practice hearing and producing final *L* in the contracted form of *will* (as in *I'll*).

In many ESL/EFL pronunciation courses, primary attention is given to contrasting the sounds *R* /r/ and *L*, as students from many language backgrounds have difficulty distinguishing these sounds. However, since many students have already experienced frustration trying to hear or make this distinction, it can be helpful instead to contrast *L* and *R* with other sounds, giving students a new perspective. In Unit 11, *R* is compared with the now familiar *D*.

 A Final sounds D and L

1. It is important to give students enough time to think about these pictures and try to feel the sound in their own mouths. They may find it helpful to look at the photographs of the wax models in Appendix B of the Student's Book and compare with these line drawings. After students have looked at the pictures, draw their attention to the blue airflow at the front of the mouth for the sound *L*. The back of the tongue is low so that air can continue to flow through these openings at either side of the tip of the tongue.

---

9 Final sounds D and L Linking with L

How do you spell "whale"?
What does "paid" mean?

 A   Final sounds D and L

1 Look at these pictures.

Stop sound D	Continuing sound L

Looking to the front

 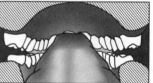

Looking down

bed   belll

Air stops   Air continues

Although it is true that many English speakers do not touch the tip of the tongue to the tooth ridge (alveolar ridge) for the word-final *L* sound, learners will have an easier time making this sound clearly if they touch the tooth ridge for both initial and final *L*.

2 Listen for the sound at the end of each word.
Do not say the words.

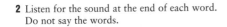

1. food	fool
food	foolll
2. made	mail
made	mailll
3. road	roll
road	rollll
4. feed	feel
feed	feelll
5. bed	bell
bed	bellll

 **B** *Which word is different?*

1 Listen. Mark the different word.

	X	Y	Z	
1.			✔	(food, food, fool)
2.	✓			
3.			✓	
4.			✓	
5.		✓		
6.			✓	
7.	✓			
8.			✓	

2 Listen again.

Unit 9 • **61**

---

with the *d* in red chalk and the *l* in purple. Then have students suggest other words with final *D* and *L* sounds to go below these key words. Include any word with a final *D* or *L* sound even if it is spelled with a silent letter *e* at the end (as in *purple*). Students can make their own charts, switching from using a pencil to using a red or purple marker when they get to the final letter.

This kinesthetic activity helps students focus on these two final sounds. This is especially helpful for students from languages that tend not to have final consonants.

 **B** *Which word is different?*

Audio script

1. food, food, fool
   /fuːd/, /fuːd/, /fuːl/

2. bell, bed, bed
   /bel/, /bed/, /bed/

3. tile, tile, tide
   /taɪl/, /taɪl/, /taɪd/

4. road, road, roll
   /roʊd/, /roʊd/, /roʊl/

5. paid, pail, paid
   /peɪd/, /peɪl/, /peɪd/

6. made, made, mail
   /meɪd/, /meɪd/, /meɪl/

7. seed, seal, seal
   /siːd/, /siːl/, /siːl/

8. feed, feed, feel
   /fiːd/, /fiːd/, /fiːl/

---

2. It can be helpful to first present the task with the words covered so that students just rely on their ears. This helps overcome interference from difficulties with identifying letters with sounds. Have students listen to the pairs again while looking at the words. Point out the stop sign and arrow sign that are again being used to represent the concepts of stop sound and continuing sound.

 **Teaching Tip**

Another way to help focus attention on the final sounds *D* and *L* is to make lists of words that end in these sounds with the letters *d* and *l* written in colored chalk. Use red for *d* because the word *red* ends in a final *D* sound and purple for *l* because the word *purple* ends in an *L* sound. Write the words *red* and *purple* on the board

🎧 **C** **Which word do you hear?**

To give students a chance to work in a more active mode, you might ask them to listen to each word and say *stop* and *continue*. Or, they could hold up a hand for *stop* or draw a continuing line in the air for *continue*.

Audio script

1. made	/meɪd/
2. fool	/fuːl/
3. roll	/roʊl/
4. bed	/bed/
5. paid	/peɪd/
6. tile	/taɪl/
7. fade	/feɪd/
8. feel	/fiːl/

🎧 **D** **Saying final sounds D and L**

It is helpful to have students practice whispering these words before they say them aloud. Whispering helps students establish an acoustic image of the sounds they are trying to produce, which is an important step in the process of learning to articulate new sounds. Whispering also changes the atmosphere in a class and can make the task more intriguing. Demonstrate whispering and let students experiment for a bit before doing the full exercise.

🎧 **E** **Music of English**

Use choral responses alternated with individual recitations of these two questions. Saturation repetition of these little "songs" can help bond the rhythm and melody to the phrase.

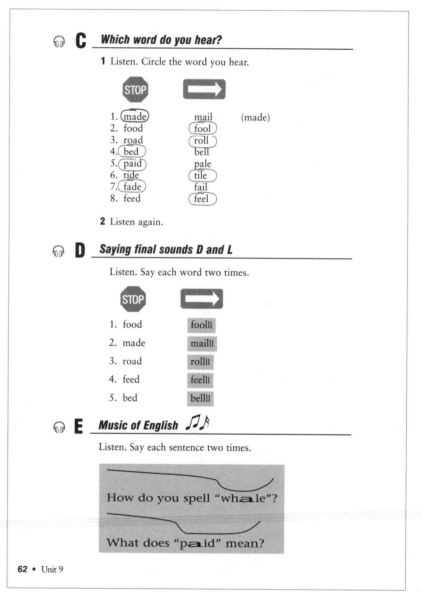

🎧 **C** Which word do you hear?

1 Listen. Circle the word you hear.

1. (made)   mail   (made)
2. food   (fool)
3. road   (roll)
4. (bed)   bell
5. (paid)   pale
6. tide   (tile)
7. (fade)   fail
8. feed   (feel)

2 Listen again.

🎧 **D** Saying final sounds D and L

Listen. Say each word two times.

1. food   foolll
2. made   mailll
3. road   rollll
4. feed   feelll
5. bed   bellll

🎧 **E** Music of English 🎵♪

Listen. Say each sentence two times.

How do you spell "whale"?

What does "paid" mean?

62 • Unit 9

💡 **Teaching Tip**

Prepare an amusing visual display to help students with the distinction between *D* and *L*. Use a wide marker to draw a face profile with an open mouth on white poster board. Cut out the mouth part. Then for the tongue, put a pink or red sock on one hand. Hold the poster up with the other hand so that the class can see the face with the opening, and hold the "sock hand" behind the mouth opening, where it can be seen. Form it into the correct tongue position for *D* as seen from the side (touching the tooth ridge and humped up towards the roof of the mouth) behind the poster. Say *bed*. Then lower your hand, with the tip of the fingers just touching the roof of the mouth behind the front teeth, and say *bell*. You can add to the image by blowing air over your

F *Pair work: Hearing and saying final D and L*

1 Student A, ask question **a** or **b**.

2 Student B, answer.

3 Student A, if the answer is correct, say "Right." If it is wrong, ask again.

4 Take turns asking questions.

Examples

> Student A: How do you spell "made"?
> Student B: M - A - I - L.
> Student A: No, "made."
> Student B: M - A - D - E.
>
> Student B: What does "fool" mean?
> Student A: A silly person.
> Student B: Right.

1. a. How do you spell "made"? M - A - D - E.
   b. How do you spell "mail"? M - A - I - L.

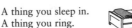

2. a. What does "food" mean? Something to eat.
   b. What does "fool" mean? A silly person.

3. a. How do you spell "road"? R - O - A - D.
   b. How do you spell "roll"? R - O - L - L.

4. a. What does "bed" mean? A thing you sleep in.
   b. What does "bell" mean? A thing you ring.

5. a. How do you spell "bed"? B - E - D.
   b. How do you spell "bell"? B - E - L - L.

6. a. What does "whale" mean? A very big sea animal.
   b. What does "wade" mean? To walk in water.

7. a. How do you spell "whale"? W - H - A - L - E.
   b. How do you spell "wade"? W - A - D - E.

hand for the continuant sound *L*. Many sounds can be demonstrated with this sock-tongue.

F *Pair work: Hearing and saying final D and L*

Many of these words may be unfamiliar, which makes them good practice material for these useful questions. Before beginning, point to each picture and have students repeat the words (*mail, roll, bed, bell, whale, wade*). After pair practice, work as a class and ask individual students the questions.

⌇ *Teaching Tip*

Give students a homework assignment to "look for" two words, one ending in *D* and one ending in *L*. Asking for only two words makes this an easy assignment, but it will encourage them to start paying attention outside of class. They can bring these words to the next class and add them to a color-coded list. (See Teaching Tip under task A on T-61.) Any activity that makes them focus on these final sounds will be of special help to students who tend to drop final consonants.

🎧 G *Listening for final L: Present or future?*

This is meant not as a grammar lesson but to increase students' awareness that the final *L* sound can make a difference in meaning by signaling future tense.

Going to as a form of the future was reviewed in Unit 7, tasks J through M. *Will*, and especially the final *L* that is a reduced form of this marker for future tense, is harder to hear. Therefore, it is important to listen for this sound to improve listening comprehension.

Audio script

> 1. I'll read the newspaper.
> 2. I'll drink coffee.
> 3. I drive to work.
> 4. I'll take the train.
> 5. We'll ride the bus.
> 6. They go home.
> 7. We watch TV.
> 8. They'll go to the movies.

8. a. What does "feed" mean? To give food.
   b. What does "feel" mean? To touch something.

9. a. How do you spell "feed"? F - E - E - D.
   b. How do you spell "feel"? F - E - E - L.

10. a. What does "paid" mean? The past of "pay."
    b. What does "pail" mean? A bucket.

🎧 G Listening for final L: Present or future?

1 Cover the sentences. Listen. Mark if the sentence is present or future.

2 Look at the sentences. Listen again.

	Present	Future
1. a. I read the newspaper. b. I'll read the newspaper.		✔
2. a. I drink coffee. b. I'll drink coffee.		✔
3. a. I drive to work. b. I'll drive to work.	✔	
4. a. I take the train. b. I'll take the train.		✔
5. a. We ride the bus. b. We'll ride the bus.		✔
6. a. They go home. b. They'll go home.	✔	
7. a. We watch TV. b. We'll watch TV.	✔	
8. a. They go to the movies. b. They'll go to the movies.		✔

H *Pair work: Present or future?*

1 Listen. Say these words two times.

Present	Future
every day	tomorrow
every night	tonight
every week	next week

2 Student A, say sentence **a** or **b**.

3 Student B, say an answer from the box above.

4 Take turns saying sentences.

Examples

Student A: We eat cake.
Student B: Every night.

Student B: We'll ask questions.
Student A: Tonight.

1. a. We eat cake.
   b. We'll eat cake.

2. a. We ask questions.
   b. We'll ask questions.

3. a. They cut the bread.
   b. They'll cut the bread.

4. a. They go to the store.
   b. They'll go to the store.

5. a. I buy fish.
   b. I'll buy fish.

6. a. I cook dinner.
   b. I'll cook dinner.

7. a. We read the newspaper.
   b. We'll read the newspaper.

8. a. We work hard.
   b. We'll work hard.

Unit 9 • **65**

H *Pair work: Present or future?*

As with previous pair work tasks, go over the examples with the class before they practice in pairs. After pair work, gather the class together and have individual students read and respond to the statements.

If students are ready for more of a challenge, have them use other expressions of time (e.g., *next Friday, each morning, after this week*, etc.). Write these expressions on the board. To model, have students read different sentences from the task, and you respond using the new expressions on the board. Then have students practice in pairs.

🎧 I *Linking with L*

It helps some students to link their fingers together while saying the linking sound. Physical gestures can be powerful reminders of abstract concepts.

🎧 J *Review: Counting syllables in sentences*

Syllable number should be reviewed often, as it needs repeated reinforcement. Awareness of syllables is essential for correct rhythm, and it can also have an important effect on grammatical accuracy of students' speech and writing. Students who have not learned to attend to the number of syllables in an utterance are more likely to miss the small structure words (e.g., prepositions, auxiliary verbs, articles, etc.) that are pronounced less clearly in natural spoken English. These students will tend to leave these important words out of their own speech and writing as well.

See Unit 9 Quiz on page T-139.

🎧 I *Linking with L*

L is a continuing sound. A continuing sound links to another continuing sound or a vowel sound at the beginning of the next word.

1 Listen.

Sell it.   Selllit .

Tell me.   Telllme .

2 Listen. Say each sentence two times.

1. Sell it now.   Selllit now.
2. Tell us everything.   Tellllus everything.
3. Do you feel okay?   Do you feelllokay ?
4. Will you go?   Willllyou go?
5. How do you spell "whale?"   How do you spellllwhale ?
6. These books are all new.   These books are allllnew .
7. Tell me all you know.   Telllme allllyou know.
8. Tom will look for the key.   Tom willlllook for the key.

🎧 J *Review: Counting syllables in sentences* ☐ ☐ ☐

1 Cover the sentences.

2 Listen. Say each sentence.

3 Write the number of syllables.

    1. Make a bowl of rice.   1. _5_
    2. We need two plates.   2. _4_
    3. They like ice cubes.   3. _4_
    4. Joe needed five tickets.   4. _6_
    5. We cleaned the plates.   5. _4_

4 Read the sentences aloud. Check your answers.

66 • Unit 9

10 Final sounds L and LD
Linking with all the stop sounds

Did you say "coal"? No, I said "cold."

🎧 A   *Final Sounds L and LD*

Listen to the final sounds in these words.

1. call	called
2. pull	pulled
3. mail	mailed
4. bowl	bold
5. sail	sailed
6. fill	filled
7. coal	cold

🎧 B   *Present and past*

1 Read the sentences.

2 Cover the sentences.

3 Listen. Mark Past or Present.

		Present	Past	
1.	I called a friend.	1.	✔	(called)
2.	I sail a boat on Sundays.	2. ✓		
3.	We mail a letter every day.	3. ✓		
4.	We mailed everything.	4.	✓	
5.	We fill our glasses.	5. ✓		
6.	A cow made our milk.	6.	✓	
7.	We sealed all the letters.	7.	✓	

4 Look at the sentences. Listen again.

Unit 10 • **67**

---

pronunciation with the accurate model. This is one of the most important reasons to encourage students to listen without repeating during the early learning of a new sound.

Note: Help students notice that these are all one-syllable words. This activity reminds them to use their ears to determine the number of syllables, rather than depending on their eyes.

💡 Teaching Tip

Another approach is to ask students to circle each word as they hear it. Or you could have them make the hand gestures for *stop* and *continue*.

🎧 B   *Present and past*

Here students listen to determine whether the sentences they hear are in the present or past tense, by focusing on the final *L* and *LD* sounds. Give students a minute or two to read the sentences. Then have them cover the sentences with their hands or a piece of paper as they listen and mark the sentences present or past. Then have them listen again while looking at the sentences.

---

10 Final sounds L and LD Linking with all the stop sounds

Unit overview

In this unit, learners focus on the distinction between the word-final sounds *L* and *LD* (/l/ and /ld/), particularly in the context of verbs, where the distinction can signal the difference between present and past tense. Students also practice confirming whether

the word they heard was correct, and linking all the English stop sounds (*T/D*, *B/P*, and *K/G*) to vowels.

🎧 A   *Final sounds L and LD*

As students listen to the audio program, remind them not to repeat the words. If they are really anxious to speak, ask them to whisper only, so that they do not confuse their own

C Pair work: What does "mail" mean?

Here students ask each other questions to test how clearly they pronounce the final *L* and *LD* sounds.

Go over the instructions and examples with students. Use the illustrations provided to help them understand new vocabulary. Tell them not to worry if there are still other words they don't know in this task. Some of the vocabulary may be unfamiliar, but that makes these questions appropriate.

Remind students to choose **a** or **b** questions at random to keep the activity challenging.

C Pair work: What does "mail" mean?

1 Student A, ask question **a** or **b**.

2 Student B, answer.

3 Take turns asking questions.

Examples

Student A: What does "mail" mean?
Student B: Things like letters and postcards.

Student B: What does "pulled" mean?
Student A: The past of "pull."

1. a. What does "made" mean?   The past of "make."
   b. What does "mail" mean?   Things like letters and postcards.

2. a. What does "pull" mean?   The opposite of "push."
   b. What does "pulled" mean?   The past of "pull."

3. a. What does "feel" mean?   To touch.
   b. What does "field" mean?   Open land.

4. a. How do you spell "while"?   W - H - I - L - E.
   b. How do you spell "wild"?   W - I - L - D.

5. a. What does "sold" mean?   The past of "sell."
   b. What does "sole" mean?   The bottom of a shoe.

6. a. What does "goal" mean?   Winning a point in soccer.
   b. What does "gold" mean?   A yellow metal.

7. a. What does "coal" mean?   A black rock that burns.
   b. What does "cold" mean?   The opposite of "hot."

8. a. What does "mild" mean?   Not strong.
   b. What does "mile" mean?   Five thousand two hundred and eighty feet.

9. a. How do you spell "smile"?   S - M - I - L - E.
   b. How do you spell "smiled"?   S - M - I - L - E - D.

10. a. What does "smiled" mean?   The past of "smile."
    b. What does "smile" mean?   To turn up your lips.

🎧 **D** **_Pair work: Present and past_**

1 Listen. Say these words two times.

Present	Past
every day	yesterday
every week	last week
usually	last year
often	two days ago
always	last night

2 Student A, say sentence **a** or **b**.

3 Student B, say an answer from the box above.

4 Take turns saying sentences.

Examples

Student A: I call home.
Student B: Every day.

Student B: We filled the gas tank.
Student A: Yesterday.

1. a. I called home.
   b. I call home.

2. a. We filled the gas tank.
   b. We fill the gas tank.

3. a. We sail on the lake.
   b. We sailed on the lake.

4. a. Babies spill milk.
   b. Babies spilled milk.

5. a. The boys fail every test.
   b. The boys failed every test.

6. a. They smile a lot.
   b. They smiled a lot.

7. a. I mailed a letter.
   b. I mail a letter.

8. a. They spelled all the words.
   b. They spell all the words.

Unit 10 • **69**

🎧 **D** **_Pair work: Present and past_**

This task gives learners more practice in clearly pronouncing the final _L_ and _LD_ sounds. It also introduces some useful time expressions.

Have students listen to the audio program and repeat the time expressions at least two times. Note that the _t_ is silent in _often_ in North American English (/ɔːf•ən/).

Go over the instructions and examples with students before having them do the pair work.

If possible, have students change partners two or three times. If students all belong to the same first language group, this kind of pair work may not work as well as in a multilingual class because the students may use non-English cues to signal a difficult sound (e.g., extra tension in their voice or body for the sound students know is

extra difficult). Even in this situation, the practice is useful because it helps focus on the final consonant and the fact that it makes a difference to meaning.

Teaching Tip

After students finish D, have them think of two or three words that can be substituted in each of these sentences, which you can then put on the board. Some words will have a comical effect. Then have the students do the task again, using these substitute words in the past/present pairs.

Examples

1. I call(ed) { a doctor. / a taxi. / an elephant.
2. We fill(ed) { the box. / our glasses. / the shop with noise.
3. We sail(ed) { on the sea. / our toy boats. / in a bathtub.
4. Babies spill(ed) { juice. / water. / everything.
5. The boys fail(ed) { the exam. / math. / to win a prize.
6. I mail(ed) { a postcard. / a box. / a cat.
7. They spell(ed) { everything / big words / their names } wrong.

T-69

🎧 **E** *Music of English*

Have students move their heads to match the pitch lines of these two sentences. This can be a slight movement or a big comical one, but the point is that, in English, gestural emphasis goes with voice emphasis.

Note: After students listen to the audio program and repeat the sentences, have them repeat the exchange at least once more as a whole piece, to show how the meanings and intonation of the sentences are linked.

F *Pair work: Did you say "made"?*

Go over the instructions and examples with your students. This task asks students to pretend that they misheard a word. If doing so makes them uneasy, explain that it is an opportunity to practice verifying information when they are not sure what was just said.

🎧 **E** Music of English ♪♪

Listen. Say each sentence two times.

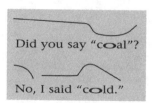

Did you say "coal"?

No, I said "cold."

F Pair work: Did you say "made"?

1 Student A, say a word from the Words box below.

2 Student B, pretend you heard a different word and ask, "Did you say ....?"

3 Student A, correct Student B and answer, "No, I said ...."

4 Take turns saying words.

Examples

> Student A: Mail.
> Student B: Did you say "made"?
> Student A: No, I said "mail."
>
> Student B: Field.
> Student A: Did you say "feel"?
> Student B: No, I said "field."

Words

mail	made	feel	field
spell	spelled	bowl	bold
pull	pulled	while	wild
sail	sailed	goal	gold

G *Linking stop sounds to vowels*

In English, the stop sounds are **T/D**, **B/P**, and **K/G**.
A stop sound links to a vowel at the beginning
of the next word.

1 Listen to the stop sounds **T** and **D**. Say each sentence
two times.

1. We paid it.   We paidit .
2. Sit on it.   Siton it.
3. Hold it.   Holdit .
4. Find it.   Findit .
5. Is it cold or hot?   Is it coldor hot?
6. We had a lot of money.   We hada lotof money.

2 Listen to the stop sounds **B**, **P**, **K**, and **G**. Say each sentence
two times.

1. The taxicab is coming.   The taxicabis coming.
2. I want a tub of butter.   I want a tubof butter.
3. Ask everybody.   Askeverybody .
4. Cook all the food.   Cookall the food.
5. Thank you.   Thankyou .
6. Help us.   Helpus .
7. Link all vowels.   Linkall vowels.
8. A cup of coffee, please.   A cupof coffee, please.
9. Stop it.   Stopit .
10. Tap each syllable.   Tapeach syllable.
11. We keep all mail.   We keepall mail.
12. This is a bag of oranges.   This is a bagof oranges.

G *Linking stop sounds to vowels*

A stop sound at the end of a word, coming before a word that begins with a vowel, "moves" to join the vowel and thus sounds like the beginning of the next word. This can make what sounds like a completely different word, as in the examples:

Examples

> *Cold ice* sounds like *coal dice*.
>
> *Paid Ann* sounds like *Pay Dan*.

It can be helpful to write these examples on the board to help students exaggerate the links as they repeat them.

See Unit 10 Quiz on page T-140.

11 Final sounds T/D and R Linking with R

Unit overview

In this unit, learners contrast the final stop sound T/D (/t/ and /d/) with the final sound R /r/, a continuing sound. R is a challenging sound for students, perhaps stemming from confusion about the letter r used to represent it. In other languages, this letter may be pronounced with a tap of the tongue on the roof of the mouth (or a flap backwards, or a trill). To an English speaker, this can sound like a stop and may be misinterpreted as a D /d/.

The main feature of the sound represented by the letter r in North American English is that it is a continuing sound. For students who tend to pronounce r with a stop quality, the combination of $R + D$ is especially difficult and can cause a loss of the past tense grammar signal in words that end in RD, for example *feared*.

🎧 A Final sounds T/D and R

1. Before students listen to the audio program, have them look at and compare the illustrations for T/D and R. They need to notice that R is a continuing sound.

---

11 Final sounds T/D and R Linking with R

What is it? Where is it?

🎧 A Final sounds T/D and R

1 Look at these pictures.

Stop sound T/D   Continuing sound R

Looking to the front

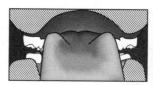 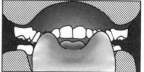

Looking down

 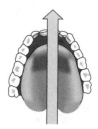

Looking to the side

bet   bed   bearrr

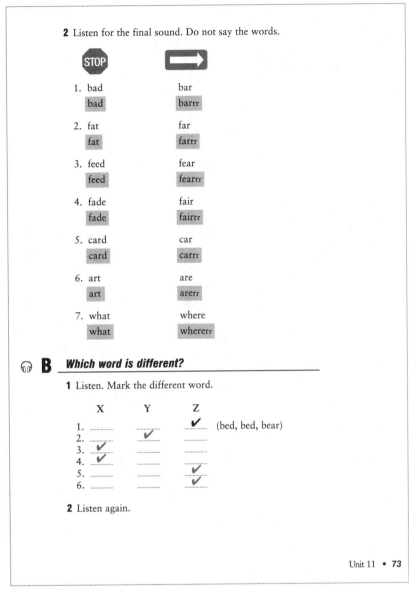

2 Listen for the final sound. Do not say the words.

STOP   →

STOP	→
1. bad	bar
bad	barrr
2. fat	far
fat	farrr
3. feed	fear
feed	fearrr
4. fade	fair
fade	fairrr
5. card	car
card	carrr
6. art	are
art	arerr
7. what	where
what	whererr

B *Which word is different?*

1 Listen. Mark the different word.

	X	Y	Z	
1.			✔	(bed, bed, bear)
2.		✔		
3.	✔			
4.	✔			
5.			✔	
6.			✔	

2 Listen again.

2. Have students make the hand gestures for *stop* and *continue* as they listen. Remind them not to repeat the words just yet. If they are really anxious to speak, ask them to whisper only.

B *Which word is different?*

Here students listen for the distinction between the final sounds *T*/*D* and *R*.

Have them listen to the audio program and put a checkmark for the words that are different.

The *R* sound can affect the vowel sound that comes before it. That is why the vowels in words like *bar* and *bad* do not sound exactly the same. But from the learner's point of view, the stop or continuant quality of the final consonant is the crucial distinction.

Audio script

1. bed, bed, bear
   /bed/, /bed/, /ber/
2. bar, bad, bar
   /bar/, /bæd/, /bar/
3. what, where, where
   /wʌt/, /wer/, /wer/
4. fired, fire, fire
   /faɪrd/, /faɪr/, /faɪr/
5. car, car, card
   /kar/, /kar/, /kard/
6. share, share, shared
   /ʃer/, /ʃer/, /ʃerd/

C Which word do you hear?

Here students listen for the distinction between final *T/D* and *R* sounds. Have them listen to the audio program and circle the words that they hear.

Audio script

1. bed	/bed/
2. are	/ɑr/
3. card	/kɑrd/
4. shared	/ʃerd/
5. fire	/fɑɪr/
6. where	/wer/
7. car	/kɑr/
8. feared	/fɪrd/
9. bad	/bæd/
10. feet	/fiːt/

D Saying final sounds T/D and R

Now student practice saying the final *T/D* and *R* sounds they have been hearing. Have them listen to the words on the audio program and repeat them at least two times.

Teaching Tip

To help students say the difficult final cluster *R + D* (*card, shared*), have them ~~practice joining two words that~~ make this cluster where they join. Ask students to repeat these phrases several times:

Examples

car door
her doll
their dog
far down

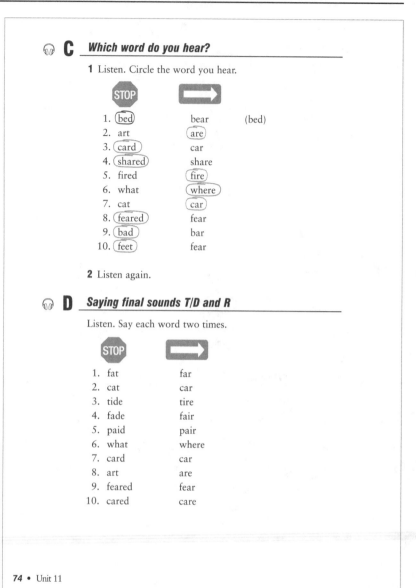

C Which word do you hear?

1 Listen. Circle the word you hear.

STOP →

	STOP	→	
1.	(bed)	bear	(bed)
2.	art	(are)	
3.	(card)	car	
4.	(shared)	share	
5.	fired	(fire)	
6.	what	(where)	
7.	cat	(car)	
8.	(feared)	fear	
9.	(bad)	bar	
10.	(feet)	fear	

2 Listen again.

D Saying final sounds T/D and R

Listen. Say each word two times.

STOP →

	STOP	→
1.	fat	far
2.	cat	car
3.	tide	tire
4.	fade	fair
5.	paid	pair
6.	what	where
7.	card	car
8.	art	are
9.	feared	fear
10.	cared	care

74 • Unit 11

E *Pair work: Present and past*

Present		Past	
every day	often	yesterday	two days ago
every week	always	last week	last night
usually		last year	

1 Student A, say sentence **a** or **b**.

2 Student B, say an answer from the box above.

3 Take turns saying sentences.

Examples

Student A: They shared everything.	Student B: I care about my work.
Student B: Yesterday.	Student A: Always.

1. a. They share everything.
   b. They shared everything.

2. a. I care about my work.
   b. I cared about my work.

3. a. They prepare their lessons.
   b. They prepared their lessons.

4. a. They feared everything.
   b. They fear everything.

5. a. We repaired cars.
   b. We repair cars.

6. a. Snakes scared me.
   b. Snakes scare me.

7. a. I adore her.
   b. I adored her.

8. a. Lions roar.
   b. Lions roared.

Unit 11 • **75**

Examples

1. They share(d) { a pizza. / a coat. / a joke.

2. I care(d) about { you. / my work. / football.

3. They prepare(d) { a cake. / a lesson. / a mistake.

4. They fear(ed) { cats. / cars. / mice.

5. We repair(ed) { clocks. / glasses. / broken hearts.

6. Snakes scare(d) { birds. / dogs. / me.

7. I adore(d) { chocolate cake. / apple pie. / you.

8. Lions roar(ed) at { animals. / trucks. / people.

E *Pair work: Present and past*

Go over the time expressions in the box with your students. It can be useful to have them repeat the expressions in unison several times. These expressions were introduced in Unit 10, but they are very useful and often confused. Then go over the instructions and examples. Remind students to choose **a** or **b** statements at random and to vary their responses.

This task helps students to see the important relationship between word-final sounds and grammatical meaning.

💡 *Teaching Tip*

As in the Teaching Tip on page T-69, have students think of other words to use in these sentences. A lively class can be creative with this task by repeating it using unlikely words.

🎧 F Linking with R

Linking practice is a good way to work on a difficult sound like *R*, because it may be easier to say at the beginning or the end of a word, depending on the rules of students' first languages. Remind students to link their hands together while they are saying the linking sounds.

🎧 G Linking with R, T/D, and L

This task aims to integrate the linking skills students practiced in the previous task with the linking with *L* they practiced in Unit 9 and the linking with *T/D* they practiced in Unit 8.

Because the *R*, *T/D*, and *L* linking sounds may sound similar in students' first languages, remind them to listen carefully for the differences between these sounds. Then play the audio program and have students repeat the sentences at least two times.

🎧 F Linking with R ⛓⛓⛓⛓⛓

R is a continuing sound. It links to a vowel or another continuing sound at the beginning of the next word.

1 Listen. Say these words two times.

far away	farrraway
hear me	hearrrme
Peter knows	Peterrrknows

2 Listen. Say each sentence two times.

1. He is far away. — He's farrraway .
2. Where is it? — Whererris it?
3. What are all those things? — What arerrall those things?
4. Peter knows the answer. — Peterrrknows the answer.
5. Did you hear me? — Did you hearrrme ?
6. Are many people going? — Arerrmany people going?
7. Her voice is beautiful. — Herrrvoice is beautiful.
8. You're an hour late. — Yourerran hourrrlate .

🎧 G Linking with R, T/D, and L ⛓⛓⛓⛓⛓

Listen. Say each sentence two times.

1. I had a sandwich. — I hada sandwich.
2. Will everybody come? — Willlleverybody come?
3. Where are you? — Whererrarerryou ?
4. What is it? — Whatis it?
5. I heard everything. — I heardeverything .
6. Is it hard or soft? — Is it hardor soft?
7. The letter never arrived. — The letterrrneverrrarrived .
8. Jill is reading. — Jilllllis reading.
9. We care about our work. — We carerraboutrrourrrwork .
10. Put your hat on. — Put your haton .

H Pair work: What does "roar" mean?

1 Student A, ask question **a** or **b**.

2 Student B, answer.

3 Student A, if the answer is correct, say "Right." If it is wrong, ask again.

4 Take turns asking questions.

Examples

Student A: What does "roared" mean?
Student B: The past of "roar."
Student A: Right.

Student B: What does "adore" mean?
Student A: The past of "love."
Student B: No. What does "adore" mean?
Student A: Love.

1. a. What does "roar" mean?   The noise of a lion.
   b. What does "roared" mean?   The past of "roar."

2. a. What does "adore" mean?   Love.
   b. What does "adored" mean?   The past of "love."

3. a. What does "repair" mean?   To fix.
   b. What does "repaired" mean?   The past of "repair."

4. a. How do you spell "feared"?   F - E - A - R - E - D.
   b. How do you spell "fear"?   F - E - A - R.

5. a. How do you spell "art"?   A - R - T.
   b. How do you spell "are"?   A - R - E.

6. a. What does "pair" mean?   Two.
   b. What does "paid" mean?   The past of "pay."

7. a. How do you spell "her"?   H - E - R.
   b. How do you spell "hurt"?   H - U - R - T.

8. a. What does "near" mean?   Not far.
   b. What does "neat" mean?   Not messy.

H Pair work: What does "roar" mean?

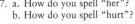

Go over the instructions and examples with your students. Then have them do the exercise in pairs. Remind them to select **a** or **b** statements at random. Use the illustrations provided to help them understand new vocabulary.

Note: As mentioned on page T-73, the *R* sound has an effect on the previous vowel, so that *pair* /per/ and *paid* /peɪd/ have rather different vowel qualities. On the other hand, the words *her* /hɜʀ/ and *hurt* /hɜrt/ have different vowel letters but the same vowel sound, which tends to bother students. Urge them to rely on their ears, not their eyes, and remind them to pay special attention to the final sound.

I Music of English

Working with *what* /wʌt/ and *where* /wer/ reinforces the work students have been doing on learning to distinguish final *T/D* and *R*. *What* and *Where* also have different vowel sounds (/wʌt/, /wer/), but it is more important for students to concentrate on the final consonant difference.

J Pair work: What is it? Where is it?

Have students first quickly read the two lists in the boxes headed *What?* and *Where?* on page 79. Practice any words you think may be new for students by pointing to the relevant picture and asking, *What is it?* or *Where is it?* Then go over the instructions and examples with your students and have them do the exercise in pairs.

---

9. a. How do you spell "fire"? F - I - R - E.
   b. How do you spell "fight"? F - I - G - H - T.

10. a. How do you spell "tire"? T - I - R - E.
    b. How do you spell "tight"? T - I - G - H - T.

I Music of English ♫♪

Listen. Say each sentence two times. Be careful with the final sound of "where" and "what."

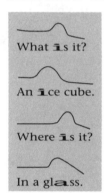

What is it?

An ice cube.

Where is it?

In a glass.

J Pair work: What is it? Where is it?

1 Student A, point to a picture on the next page and ask, "What is it?" or "Where is it?"

2 Student B, say an answer from the box on the next page.

3 Take turns asking questions.

Examples

> Student A: (Point to elephant.) What is it?
> Student B: An elephant.
>
> Student B: Where is it?
> Student A: In a zoo.

What?	Where?
A cat.	On a chair.
An elephant.	Under a sofa.
An ice cube.	On a desk.
A flag.	On a flagpole.
A jacket.	In a zoo.
A pot.	In a glass.
A computer.	On a stove.

K *Music of English* ♫♪

Listen. Say each sentence two times.

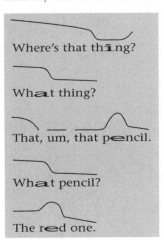

Where's that th**ī**ng?

Wh**a**t thing?

That, um, that p**e**ncil.

Wh**a**t pencil?

The r**e**d one.

Unit 11 • **79**

K *Music of English*

Ask students if they ever have trouble remembering the word for something in their own language, and if so, what general words they use instead. Tell them that, in English, the general words *thing* and *stuff* are useful for people with limited vocabulary.

Low-level students may not be ready to understand the abstract distinction between *countable* and *noncountable* nouns (e.g., *two pencils, many books*, but *some milk, some cheese*). However, even without knowing about this difference, it is useful for them to practice questions using the words *thing* (countable) and *stuff* (uncountable).

It is quite usual to say *um* or *uh* while thinking of a word. This hesitation sound means "I am not finished speaking yet, just thinking." It holds the speaker's turn briefly and is therefore more useful than just a pause.

Note: After students listen to the audio program and repeat the sentences, have them repeat the exchange at least once more as a whole piece, to show how the meanings of the sentences are linked.

 **L** *Pair work: Asking for more information*

Have students listen to the conversation on the audio program before they practice with each other. Remind them to emphasize the words in bold.

Note: Some people say *refrigerator,* but the shorter version, *fridge* /frɪdʒ/, is quite common.

‿ᓂ́⁻ Teaching Tip

For added practice with *Where is that thing?* / *What thing?*, students could make lists of items (*book, key, hat, computer,* etc.), descriptive words (*new, yellow, plastic, metal,* etc.), and places (*kitchen, living room, office, bank*) and then make their own conversations based on this pattern.

See Unit 11 Quiz on page T-141.

L **Pair work: Asking for more information**

1 Listen.

2 Say the conversation with a partner. Take turns as Sue and Joe.

Sue: Where's my stuff?
Joe: **What** stuff?
Sue: That, um, that cheese.
Joe: **Which** cheese?
Sue: The cheese I put in the fridge.
Joe: **When**?
Sue: Last month.
Joe: Oh, **that** cheese! I threw it away!

12 Continuing sounds and stop sounds + S/Z
Linking with S/Z

What's a bank for?
Where's the library? It's on Main Street.

A Review: Final sounds T/D and S/Z

Listen. Say these words two times.

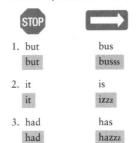

	STOP	
1.	but	bus
	but	busss
2.	it	is
	it	izzz
3.	had	has
	had	hazzz

B Do you hear a final S/Z sound?

1 Listen. Mark Yes or No.

	Yes	No	
1.	✔		(bus)
2.		✓	
3.	✓		
4.		✓	
5.		✓	
6.	✓		
7.	✓		
8.		✓	
9.		✓	
10.	✓		

2 Listen again.

Unit 12 • **81**

A Review: Final sounds T/D and S/Z

The aim of this task is to refresh students' memories of the sounds *T/D* and *S/Z* introduced in Unit 8. Have them listen to the audio program and repeat the words at least two times.

B Do you hear a final S/Z sound?

As students listen to the audio program, have them check whether they hear a final *S/Z* sound or not.

Audio script

1.	bus	/bʌs/
2.	but	/bʌt/
3.	has	/hæz/
4.	hat	/hæt/
5.	shop	/ʃɑp/
6.	shops	/ʃɑps/
7.	banks	/bæŋks/
8.	bank	/bæŋk/
9.	road	/roʊd/
10.	roads	/roʊdz/

12 Continuing sounds and stop sounds + S/Z Linking with S/Z

Unit overview

The main focus of this unit is on consonant clusters with final *S/Z*. Students will practice using and listening for *S/Z* as a plural marker for nouns and as a reduced form of *is* in *What's*, *Where's*, and *It's*.

Consonant clusters are difficult for students whose first languages do not allow consonants together. Also, in some languages, few consonants can occur in final position. This is one possible reason why the grammatically important final *S/Z* is often omitted.

Unit 12

🎧 **C** *Stop sounds + S/Z*

In this task, students listen for the *S/Z* ending after stop sounds. Remind them that final *S/Z* is the crucial sound for signaling that an item is plural.

Have students listen to the audio program and circle the words they hear.

Note: The plural ending is always spelled with the letter *s*, but it may be pronounced either as *S* or *Z*. The difference is caused by the quality of the preceding consonant. If that consonant is unvoiced, then the final letter *s* is pronounced *S* (e.g., *caps* /kæps/). However, if that consonant is voiced, then the final letter is pronounced *Z* (e.g., *cabs* /kæbz/).

It is not necessary to explain this to beginning students, as it might confuse them. At this stage it is enough to make them aware that there may be variations in sound for the letter *s*.

Audio script

1. cabs /kæbz/
2. bank /bæŋk/
3. bags /bægz/
4. stops /staps/
5. supermarket /ˈsuː•pər‚mɑr•kət/
6. laundromat /ˈlɔːn•drə‚mæt/
7. roads /roʊdz/
8. streets /striːts/
9. shop /ʃɑp/
10. parking lots /ˈpɑr•kɪŋ ‚lɑts/

🎧 **C** <u>*Stop sounds + S/Z*</u>

The English stop sounds are **T/D**, **P/B**, and **K/G**.

1 Listen. Circle the word you hear.

STOP	STOP + S/Z
1. cab cab	(cabs) cabzzz
2. (bank) bank	banks banksss
3. bag bag	(bags) bagzzz
4. stop stop	(stops) stopsss
5. (supermarket) supermarket	supermarkets supermarketsss
6. (laundromat) laundromat	laundromats laundromatsss
7. road road	(roads) roadzzz
8. street street	(streets) streetsss
9. (shop) shop	shops shopsss
10. parking lot parking lot	(parking lots) parking lotsss

2 Listen again.

82 • Unit 12

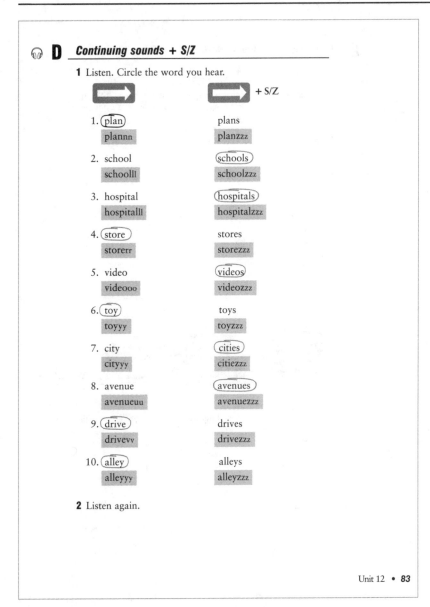

🎧 **D** _Continuing sounds + S/Z_

1 Listen. Circle the word you hear.

➡️   ➡️ + S/Z

1. (plan)   plans
   plannn   planzzz

2. school   (schools)
   schoolll   schoolzzz

3. hospital   (hospitals)
   hospitalll   hospitalzzz

4. (store)   stores
   storerr   storezzz

5. video   (videos)
   videooo   videozzz

6. (toy)   toys
   toyyy   toyzzz

7. city   (cities)
   cityyy   citiezzz

8. avenue   (avenues)
   avenueuu   avenuezzz

9. (drive)   drives
   drivevv   drivezzz

10. (alley)   alleys
    alleyyy   alleyzzz

2 Listen again.

Unit 12 • **83**

🎧 **D** _Continuing sounds + S/Z_

Now students listen for the _S/Z_ ending after continuing sounds. Have students listen to the audio program and circle the words they hear.

Note: Items **4**, **8**, and **9** have silent -_e_ endings.

Audio script

1. plan   /plæn/
2. schools   /skuːlz/
3. hospitals /ˈhɑs,pɪt•əlz/
4. store   /stɔːr/
5. videos   /ˈvɪd•iː,ouz/
6. toy   /tɔɪ/
7. cities   /ˈsɪt̮•iz/
8. avenues   /ˈæv•ə,nuːz/
9. drive   /draɪv/
10. alley   /ˈæl•i/

E Pair work: Is it one or more than one?

To introduce this task, draw a star on the left side of the board and write the word *star* above it. Ask *How many?* When a student answers *one,* write *one* beneath the star. Then draw several stars on the right side of the board and write *stars* above them. Ask *How many?* Students may tell you the number of stars; accept their answers, and write *more than one* beneath the group of stars. Remind students how important the *S* sound is in English, because it indicates more than one.

Then read the directions aloud and model the task by taking the part of Student A and choosing someone in the class to take the part of Student B. Students can repeat after you the names of the places in the box before you put them into pairs to complete the task. Use the illustrations on pages 84 and 86 to help explain what these places are.

E Pair work: Is it one or more than one?

1 Student A, say a word from the Places box.

2 Student B, if you hear a word meaning one place, hold up one finger. If you hear a word meaning more than one place, hold up all five fingers.

3 Student A, if the answer is correct, say "Right." If it is wrong, say the word again.

4 Take turns saying words.

Examples

Student A: Banks.
Student B: (Hold up all five fingers.)
Student A: Right.

Student B: Hospitals.
Student A: (Hold up one finger.)
Student B: No, "hospitals."

Places

park	parking lot	theaters	parking lots
laundromat	hospitals	school	bookstores
apartments	schools	bank	parks
toy department	drugstore	hospital	bookstore
video shop	banks	shops	

It will help students' listening comprehension if they become aware of the way English speakers systematically contract auxiliaries such as *is* in normal speech. For that reason it is useful to practice saying *what's*. However, this should be restricted to meaning "What is . . .", rather than "What does . . ." because beginning students have a tendency to say *What means that?* instead of *What does that mean?* Therefore practice with the contraction of *does* should be put off until a later stage.

Note: After students listen to the audio program and repeat the sentences, have them repeat the exchange at least once more as a whole piece, to show how the meanings and intonation patterns of the sentences are linked.

🎧 **F** ___ *Review: Linking with S/Z* ⛓

Remember that S/Z links to vowels and to other continuing sounds.

Listen. Say each sentence two times.

1. The shops are downtown.   The shopsssare downtown.
2. The roads are full of traffic.   The roadzzzare full of traffic.
3. The parking lots are full of cars.   The parking lotsssare full of cars.
4. The banks are closed today.   The banksssare closed today.
5. Are the shops open?   Are the shopsssopen ?
6. Supermarkets are always open.   Supermarketsssare alwayzzzopen .
7. The schools may be open.   The schoolzzzmay be open.
8. Taxicabs never wait here.   Taxicabzzznever wait here.
9. Toy shops sell toys.   Toy shopsssssell toys.
10. Restaurants serve food.   Restaurantsssserve food.

🎧 **G** ___ *Music of English* 🎵

Listen. Say each sentence two times. Go up or down on the most important word.

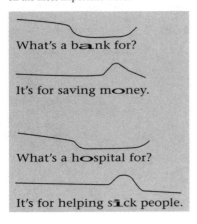

What's a bank for?

It's for saving money.

What's a hospital for?

It's for helping sick people.

🎧 **F** *Review: Linking with S/Z*

Have students listen to the audio program and repeat each sentence at least two times.

Remind students that it is important to practice linking because it will make their speech more understandable and improve their listening comprehension. Also remind them that it is necessary to be attentive about hearing and saying the final *S* sound, since it carries so much information.

🎧 **G** *Music of English*

In this task, students integrate three things they have studied:

1. consonant clusters with *S*
2. using intonation to highlight the most important word in a sentence
3. linking with *S/Z*

Have students listen to the audio program and repeat each sentence at least two times.

H Pair work: What's a bank for?

Have students repeat after you the words in the *Places* and *Answers* boxes. Remind them to pay attention to the strong syllables in the words and the most important words in the sentences. Then read the instructions, and model the task by taking the part of Student A and choosing someone in the class to take the part of Student B.

Tell students that *What's it for?* is a useful question for language learners because it gives them an easy way to find out the meaning of unknown vocabulary.

Note: Students may be confused by the similarity between *park* (the noun) and *parking*. This exercise can help them separate the meanings of the two words.

H Pair work: What's a bank for?

1 Student A, look at the Places box. Ask what one of the places is for.

2 Student B, say an answer from the Answers box.

3 Take turns asking questions.

Examples

> Student A: What's a library for?
> Student B: It's for borrowing books.
>
> Student B: What's a toy store for?
> Student A: It's for buying toys.

Places

park	supermarket	bookstore	high school
bank	toy store	restaurant	preschool
video shop	auto supply store	hardware store	post office
drugstore	library	hospital	parking lot
laundromat			

Answers

It's for eating.	It's for mail.
It's for washing clothes.	It's for saving money.
It's for buying books.	It's for renting videos.
It's for buying toys.	It's for borrowing books.
It's for buying stuff like tools.	It's for helping sick people.
It's for buying food.	It's for teenagers.
It's for buying stuff like medicine.	It's for very small children.
It's for trees and grass.	It's for buying stuff for the car.
	It's for cars.

I Music of English 🎵🎵

Listen. Say each sentence two times.

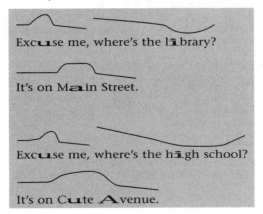

Excuse me, where's the library?

It's on Main Street.

Excuse me, where's the high school?

It's on Cute Avenue.

J Pair work: Giving locations

1 Listen. Find the places on the map.

Visitor: Excuse me, where's the bookstore?
Resident: It's on the corner of Main and Jen.
Visitor: Is it near the library?
Resident: Yes, it's just across the street.
Visitor: And where is Jen Street?
Resident: It's one block south of Jean Street.
Visitor: Thanks a lot for your help.
Resident: No problem.

2 Say the conversation with a partner. Take turns as the visitor and the resident.

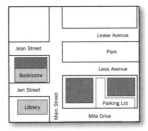

a good idea to review the words for the four directions (*north*, *south*, *east*, and *west*) represented by *N*, *S*, *E*, and *W* before moving on to the next task.

Review the Two Vowel Rule and One Vowel Rule in preparation for task K, using *Main* and *Jen* as examples. The map game on pages 88–90 presents a challenge based on these vowel rules.

Note: When giving street names, it isn't necessary to say the word *street* (e.g., *It's on the corner of Main and Jen.*).

💡 Teaching Tip

If your students are able to manage more complex directions, they should be encouraged to think of other ways to give directions.

Examples

It's six blocks to the south of _____.
It's near _____.
It's across the street from _____.
It's on the northwest corner of _____.

I Music of English

Tell students that the rest of the tasks in this unit will give them practice in asking for directions, a very useful skill in a foreign country. Have them listen to the audio program and repeat each sentence at least two times.

Note: After students listen to the audio program and repeat the sentences, have them repeat the two exchanges at least once more as whole units, to show how the meanings and intonation patterns of the sentences are linked.

J Pair work: Giving locations

Have students listen to the audio program. Then discuss the meanings of the expressions *on the corner of*, *across the street*, and *one block south* before students practice the conversation with a partner. It would be

K *Pair work: Map game*

Go over the names of the streets on the map on page 89. Then read the instructions, and model the task by taking the part of Student A and choosing someone in the class to take the part of Student B. Remind students not to look at each other's maps.

If you are teaching Spanish speakers, remind them about the number of syllables in *State* and *Street,* as they will have a tendency to add a vowel before *S* with another consonant at the beginning of a word.

💡 *Teaching Tip*

Another approach is to paint or draw a reusable map on a large piece of cloth or plastic sheeting and have students take turns giving each other directions to walk to locations. This makes an entertaining activity and reinforces the need for vowel clarity.

See Unit 12 Quiz on page T-142.

K   *Pair work: Map game*   EXTRA

1 Ask about locations. Student A looks at Map A on page 89. Student B looks at Map B on page 90.

2 Student A, ask the location of a place in the box below the map.

3 Student B, answer the question.

4 Student A, write the place on your map.

5 Take turns asking questions. When your maps are complete, check your answers.

Example

> Student A: (Look at Map A.) Where's the toy store?
> Student B: (Look at Map B.) It's on the corner of Main
> Street and Jean Street.
> Student A: (Write "toy store" on your map.)

Map A

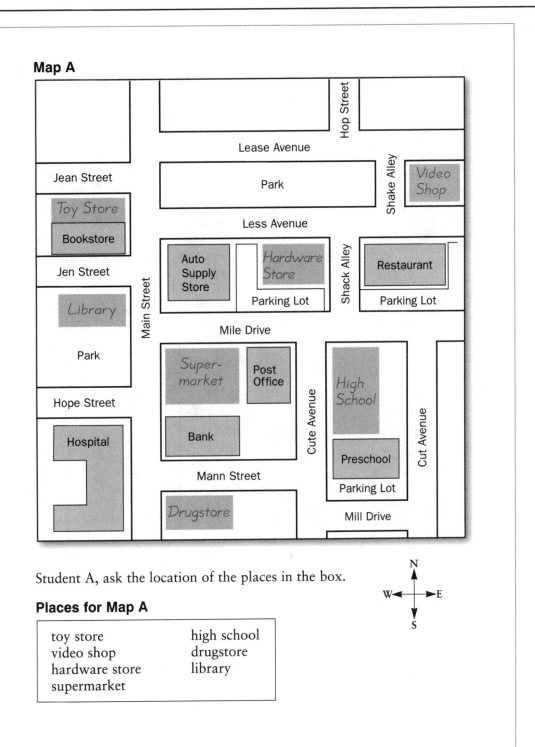

Student A, ask the location of the places in the box.

Places for Map A

toy store	high school
video shop	drugstore
hardware store	library
supermarket	

Map B

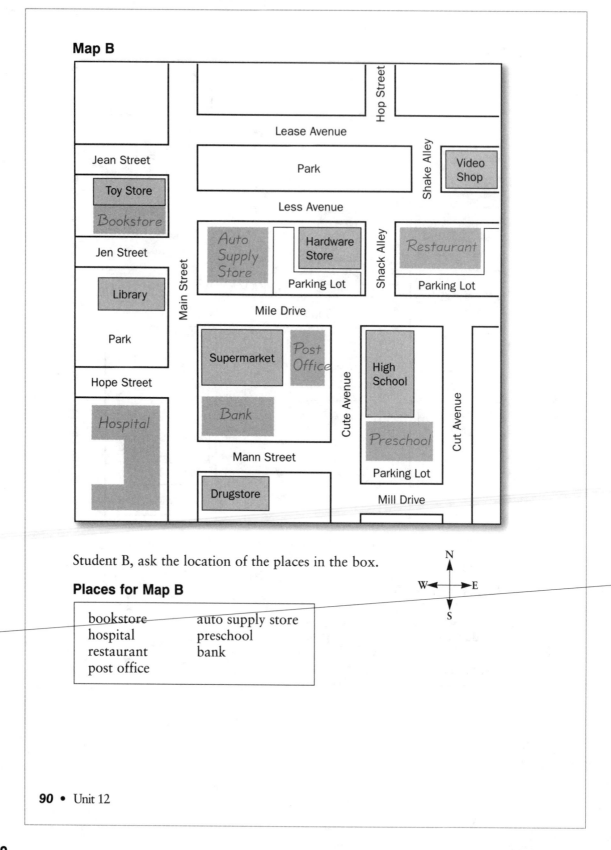

Student B, ask the location of the places in the box.

Places for Map B

bookstore	auto supply store
hospital	preschool
restaurant	bank
post office	

13 Numbers
Checking and correcting mistakes

Did you say "ninety"? No, "nineteen."
What does Shane sell?

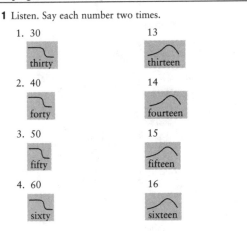

🎧 **A** *Saying numbers and years*

1 Listen. Say each number two times.

1. 30 — thirty   13 — thirteen
2. 40 — forty   14 — fourteen
3. 50 — fifty   15 — fifteen
4. 60 — sixty   16 — sixteen

2 Listen. Say each year two times.

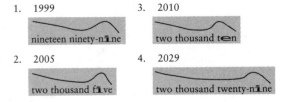

1. 1999 — nineteen ninety-nine   3. 2010 — two thousand ten
2. 2005 — two thousand five   4. 2029 — two thousand twenty-nine

---

for students, so this unit introduces a verification/correction technique to help students confirm which one was said. The same technique is then applied to phone numbers.

🎧 **A** *Saying numbers and years*

Have students listen to the audio program and repeat the numbers and years they hear at least two times. Students can trace the pitch lines in the blue boxes with their index fingers as they listen, to reinforce the difference in the intonation patterns used for numbers ending in *-ty* and *-teen*.

If you have a class of students who are roughly the same age, or for whom personal questions about age are not a problem, you can write these questions on the board and have them ask each other *How old are you?* and *What year were you born?*

---

13 Numbers
Checking and correcting mistakes

Unit overview

This very practical unit focuses on numbers. Students will practice the distinction between the often-confused *-teen* and *-y* number endings, and will practice saying telephone numbers. They will also review all of the different combinations of linking sounds they have learned so far.

Numbers are a necessary part of a new language, needed for everyday use. However, they are sometimes hard to remember because we all learned to count very early in our native language and so we tend to think numerically in that language.

Similar-sounding pairs of numbers like *thirteen* and *thirty* are especially confusing

🎧 **B** *Music of English*

Have students listen to the audio program and repeat each sentence at least two times.

Note: After students listen to the audio program and repeat the sentences, have them repeat the two exchanges at least once more as whole units, to show how the meanings and intonation patterns of the sentences are linked.

C *Pair work: Correcting a mistake about a number*

Ask students, *In what situations do you need to hear numbers correctly?* (Sample answers: at the bank, when making appointments and reservations, when shopping, etc.) Then ask, *Why is it important to check that you heard the correct number?* (Sample answers: you may lose money, you may not be able to communicate with someone, you may miss a train, etc.) Remind students not to be shy about checking numbers they are not sure about, as the consequences can be serious!

Go over the instructions and examples with students. Tell them to choose from the three columns of numbers at random to keep this task interesting. This task asks students to pretend that they misheard a number. If doing so makes them uneasy, explain that it is an opportunity to practice verifying information when they are not sure what was just said.

Note: It may be helpful to explain that boldface type in the example conversations highlights the words and syllables that receive special emphasis. In these conversations the numbers are emphasized because the speakers are asking and correcting to confirm which numbers were said.

🎧 **B** Music of English 🎵♪

Listen. Say each sentence two times.

Did you say "ninety"?

No, "nineteen."

Did you say "ninety-seven"?

No, "ninety-nine."

C **Pair work: Correcting a mistake about a number**

1 Student A, say a number from the Numbers box.

2 Student B, pretend that you did not understand. Ask about a different number.

3 Student A, correct the mistake.

4 Take turns saying the numbers.

Examples

Student A: Fifty.
Student B: Did you say "fif**teen**"?
Student A: No, "**fif**ty."
Student B: Twenty-nine.
Student A: Did you say "twenty-**five**"?
Student B: No, "twenty-**nine**."

Numbers

13	30	16
60	19	90
14	40	17
70	66	67
15	50	18
80	98	99
2018	2080	2020

🎧 **D** *Music of English* 🎵♪

Listen. Say the telephone number two times.

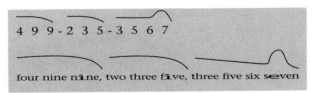

🎧 **E** *Listening for pauses in telephone numbers*

Telephone numbers are said with a pause (silence) after each group of numbers. In different countries, these groups are different.

Listen for the pauses in these telephone numbers.

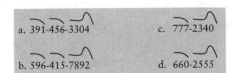

Australia	03-9568-0322
Canada	604-892-5808
Japan	03-3295-5875
Mexico	55-19-59-39
New Zealand	9-377-3800
United Kingdom	01223-325-847
United States	212-924-3900

🎧 **F** *Saying telephone numbers*

1 Listen. Say these U.S. telephone numbers two times. The first two have area codes.

a. 391-456-3304   c. 777-2340

b. 596-415-7892   d. 660-2555

2 Now dictate your own telephone number to a partner. Check what your partner wrote.

🎧 **D** *Music of English*

Have students listen to the audio program and repeat the telephone number at least two times. It can be useful to explain to students that there are conventional ways for grouping telephone numbers (as well as other numbers such as credit card account numbers), and that it is difficult for listeners to understand numbers if they are not grouped according to local conventions. Anybody who has tried to get a telephone number from an operator in a foreign country is likely to have experienced this difficulty.

🎧 **E** *Listening for pauses in telephone numbers*

Each of these telephone numbers begins with an area code. As students listen to the numbers in this task, encourage them to tap their pencils or feet at the pauses. Be sure to tell them that the hyphen (-) gives them a visual clue as to where to put the pauses.

🎧 **F** *Saying telephone numbers*

Have students listen to the audio program and repeat the telephone numbers they hear at least two times. Then have them dictate their own phone numbers to their partners and check what their partners wrote.

💡 *Teaching Tip*

If you have an out-of-date or extra telephone directory, use it to give students more practice in saying phone numbers. Simply tear out a page for each student and have them dictate three or more numbers on that page to their partners, and then check what their partners wrote.

🎧 G Stores at the Seaside Mall

This task introduces a context in which students will be able to practice saying numbers. Before students listen to the audio program, have them read the directory. The locations given tell where each store is located within the mall, including the level A, B, or C. Then have students listen to the audio program and say the name of each store two times.

Please be aware that the Seaside Mall is a fictional place. Your students should not try to call any of these numbers!

Note: The vowel letter in *mall,* /mɔːl/ does not follow the One Vowel Rule, but instead sounds like the vowel in *fall, ball, call, coffee* /ˈkɔː•fi/, *soft* /sɔːft/. This vowel sound is not included in the system of 11 vowels on which this course is based (alphabet vowels, relative vowels, and the schwa), because beginners' most urgent need is to have simple rules they can use to decode most words. Other vowels can be studied later.

🎧 **G** *Stores at the Seaside Mall*

1 Read the Seaside Mall directory below.

2 Listen. Say the name of each store two times.

SEASIDE MALL DIRECTORY

Men	Location	Phone
Mr. True	1A	214-1698
Shane	25B	213-1697

Women		
The Trap	14C	213-2134
Smart Woman	20A	214-1597

Boys		
Red Dog	16A	214-1718

Girls		
Mall Mice	17A	213-1719
California Girl	15A	213-9070

Food		
FastBurger	5B	213-1232
Sunshine Cafe	6C	213-1658
The Elephant Eatery	7B	214-2194

Other Stores		
Small World	15B	215-3200
Gemstones	13B	215-3214
Video Mania	21C	214-5599
Music Universe	31C	214-8790

94 • Unit 13

H Music of English 🎵🎵

Listen. Say each sentence two times.

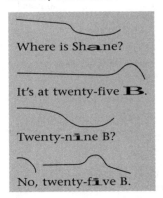

I Pair work: Calling for information

1 There are three levels at the Seaside Mall:
Level A, B, and C. Listen to this phone conversation.

2 Say the conversation two times with a partner.

Clerk: Seaside Mall. May I help you?
Customer: Yes, please. What's the telephone number
for the Sunshine Cafe?
Clerk: 213-1658.
Customer: 213-1698?
Clerk: No, 213-1658.
Customer: Okay. Where is it?
Clerk: It's at 6C.
Customer: Thanks.
Clerk: You're welcome.

intonation patterns of the
sentences are linked.

I Pair work: Calling for information

Have students listen to the
audio program and then say
the conversation at least two
times with a partner. Have
partners switch roles the
second time they practice
the conversation.

💡 Teaching Tip

This activity and the next
one can be made more
enjoyable and challenging
by having students sit back-
to-back. Encourage them to
hold imaginary telephone
receivers to their ears so that
it feels more like they are
actually having a telephone
conversation. When they
cannot see each other's
mouths, they have to rely
entirely on their ears.

H Music of English

Have students listen to the
audio program and repeat each
sentence of this conversation at
least two times.

The exchange *Where is
Shane?*/*It's at twenty-five B*
illustrates the customary
signaling of the final element of
a list of items with a lengthened
vowel and a rise-fall in the
pitch. Students learned this
pattern when they studied
spelling in Unit 4. The same
pattern is used for acronyms
(e.g., *UN, TV, BBC*, etc.) and
lists of numbers, lists of words,
or lists of any kind.

Nine and *five* are frequently
confused or misheard by
students who tend not to notice
final consonants.

Note: After students listen to
the audio program and repeat
the sentences, have them
repeat the exchange at least
once more as a whole piece, to
show how the meanings and

J Pair work: Where is it? What's the telephone number?

Go over the instructions, then model the example with someone in the class. Have students take turns being the customer and the clerk. Student A can ask for the first seven phone numbers and locations, and Student B for the second seven.

A much more difficult task could be for a student to read a telephone number aloud, asking the partner to name the store that goes with that number. This is not a realistic situation, but if the students have done the other tasks without difficulty, they might enjoy a more challenging exercise.

Teaching Tip

Here is an amusing and challenging – but very noisy – way to do this pair-work task with smaller classes. After going over the task instructions, have all Student As line up facing the right wall, and all Student Bs facing the left wall. Tell them to do the task from these positions. Students will have to speak very loudly and clearly and will have to concentrate hard on distinguishing their partner's voice. After students finish the task, let them meet with their partners to check their answers, but tell them they must check orally, without looking at each other's books.

J Pair work: Where is it? What's the telephone number?

1 Customer, look at the Places box below. (Don't look at the Seaside Mall directory.) Ask for the location and telephone number of a store.

2 Clerk, look at the directory on page 94. Answer.

3 Customer, check your answer with your partner. Then write the location and telephone number in the box.

4 Take turns as the customer and clerk at the information desk.

Example

> Customer: Excuse me, where is The Trap?
> Clerk: It's at 14C.
> Customer: Thanks. What's the phone number?
> Clerk: It's 213-2134.
> Customer: 213-2134?
> Clerk: That's right.

Places

	Location	Phone
Mr. True	1A	214-1698
Shane	25B	213-1697
The Trap	14C	213-2134
Smart Woman	20A	214-1597
Red Dog	16A	214-1718
Mall Mice	17A	213-1719
California Girl	15A	213-9070
FastBurger	5B	213-1232
Sunshine Cafe	6C	213-1658
The Elephant Eatery	7B	214-2194
Small World	15B	215-3200
Gemstones	13B	215-3214
Video Mania	21C	214-5599
Music Universe	31C	214-8790

🎧 K *About the stores at the Seaside Mall*

Listen to information about the stores at the Seaside Mall.

SEASIDE MALL		
$$$ Expensive	**$$ Moderate**	**$ Inexpensive**
$$$	The Trap	clothes for women
$	Mr. True	clothes for men
$$	Shane	clothes for men
$	Smart Woman	clothes for women
$$	Small World	toys
$$$	Gemstones	jewelry
$$	Music Universe	music CDs and tapes
$$	Video Mania	videos and video games
$$	Mall Mice	clothes for girls
$$$	California Girl	clothes for girls
$	Red Dog	clothes for boys
$$$	Sunshine Cafe	big sandwiches
$$	The Elephant Eatery	soup, salad, and pizza
$	FastBurger	burgers and ice cream

🎧 L *Music of English* 🎵

Listen. Say each sentence two times.

What does Shane sell?

Clothes for men.

Did you say clothes for teens?

No, for men.

🎧 L *Music of English*

Have students listen to the audio program and say each sentence at least two times.

Note: After students listen to the audio program and repeat the sentences, have them repeat the exchange at least once more as a whole piece, to show how the meanings and intonation patterns of the sentences are linked.

🔆 *Teaching Tip*

Try putting students in groups of four for further practice. Have two of the students say line 1 of the exchange in unison. Then have the other two students say line 2 in unison, and so on. Then they should switch roles. Speaking along with someone else can help shy students pronounce the lines more assertively.

🎧 K *About the stores at the Seaside Mall*

Ask students if they ever go to malls, and if so, what kinds of stores there are there. Then have students cover the right column of the Seaside Mall chart with a sheet of paper. Ask them to guess what each store sells. Some will be easy to guess (for example, Video Mania sells videos), but others, such as Shane and Mall Mice, may inspire some creative guessing.

Tell students you are going to play the audio program, and that they can uncover each answer in the chart *after* they hear it. Tell them that this information will prepare them to do the next two tasks.

Note: No store would advertise itself as cheap (which can imply low-quality goods), but instead might use a term like *discount,* or *factory outlet,* which implies low prices.

M Pair work: Checking information

Have students listen to the conversation on the audio program and then practice the conversation at least two times with a partner. They should switch roles the second time they practice.

Then have them take turns being the customer and asking about what some of the stores at the Seaside Mall sell. They can look at G, page 94, for a list of stores. The clerk can find the answers in K, page 97.

More advanced students might enjoy adding information about these stores (or inventing new stores) to quiz each other about.

Note: The clerk's emphasis should be on the first syllable of *inexpensive,* because that contrast is the main point of the answer.

N More linking

Start by pointing out that this task gives examples of five different categories of linking. Go over each category, eliciting examples. Then have students listen to the audio program and repeat each sentence at least two times. Point out to them the many different categories of linking that they have learned.

Note: Linking with the word *is* often results in a contraction, dropping the vowel altogether.

Examples

> Smart Woman's inexpensive.
> The Trap's expensive.

M Pair work: Checking information

1 Listen to the conversation.

2 Say the conversation two times with a partner.

Customer: What does Smart Woman sell?
   Clerk: Clothes for women.
Customer: Did you say clothes for **teens**?
   Clerk: No, for **women**.
Customer: Is it expensive?
   Clerk: No. It's **in**expensive.
Customer: Thanks.
   Clerk: You're very welcome.

3 Take turns as the customer and the clerk. Ask what a store sells and if it is expensive. Find the answers in the box in K, page 97.

N More linking

Listen. Say each sentence two times.

1. Continuing sound + vowel sound

   Smart Woman is inexpensive.   Smart Womannnizzzinexpensive .
   FastBurger opens at ten.   FastBurgerrropenzzzat ten.

2. Stop sound + vowel sound

   The Trap is closed on Sundays.   The Trapis closedon Sundays.
   Small World is fun.   Small Worldis fun.

3. Continuing sound + continuing sound

   FastBurger never costs much.   FastBurgerrrnever costs much.
   Teens like shopping.   Teenzzzlike shopping.

4. Vowel sound + vowel sound

   Mr. True is inexpensive.   Mr. Trueuuizzz inexpensive.
   Video Mania is busy.   Video Maniaaais busy.

5. Same sound to same sound

   Gemstones sells jewelry.   Gemstonessssells jewelry.
   John never buys books.   Johnnnnever buys books.

🎧 **O** *Linking with vowels* 🔗🔗🔗🔗🔗

1 Listen to the linking in these questions. Say each question two times.

2 Draw lines to link vowel sounds.

1. Are you in the movies?
2. Are you alive?
3. Are you an actor?
4. Are you on TV?
5. Did you ever play sports?
6. Who are you?

P *Twenty Questions game* | EXTRA |

Play this game with your class. Student A is a famous person. (For example, a movie star, singer, politician, or artist.) Take turns asking yes/no questions until someone guesses who Student A is. The goal is to guess who the person is in fewer than twenty questions.

Example

> Student A: (You decide to be Elvis Presley.)
> Student B: Are you alive?
> Student A: No.
> Student C: Are you a man?
> Student A: Yes.
>
> (Questions continue.)

Here are some example questions. Make up your own questions, too.

1. Are you alive?
2. Are you a man?
3. Are you an actor?
4. Are you an artist?
5. Are you a politician?
6. Do we buy your records?
7. Do we hear you on the radio?
8. Do we see you on TV?
9. Are you in the movies?
10. Were you in *Star Wars*?

Unit 13 • **99**

P *Twenty Questions game* EXTRA

Go over the instructions and example with your students. Then think of a famous person your students are likely to know and have them ask you questions first before playing the game by themselves. They can play as a whole class or in small groups. As they are playing, walk around the room and check to make sure they are linking the words in the questions.

If you think students might have a difficult time thinking of famous people, you could make several cards with the names of famous people on them. If possible, include some local or currently trendy celebrities.

See Unit 13 Quiz on page T-143.

🎧 **O** *Linking with vowels*

Each of the questions in this task includes an example of linking between a word-final vowel and a vowel at the beginning of the next word.

Have students listen to the linking in each question on the audio program and repeat at least two times.

Note: Alphabet vowels link with a following vowel by continuing their ^{y} or ^{w} offglide until the next vowel begins.

Examples

the ^{y} answer

he ^{y} asked

go ^{w} away

you ^{w} always

to ^{w} everything

who ^{w} are

T-99

14 Final sounds N, L, ND, and LD
Linking with N, L, ND, and LD

Unit overview

In this unit, students will practice distinguishing between and pronouncing the final sounds *N, L, ND,* and *LD* (/n/, /l/, /nd/, /ld/). They will also work on linking with these sounds, and practice checking and correcting information.

A Final sounds N, L, and D

For students from some language backgrounds, it is difficult to learn to make the difference between *N, L,* and *D.* Before teaching this unit, take some time to use a mirror (and perhaps a flashlight) to look into your own mouth. You will see the soft part of the roof of your mouth hanging down at the back. This is the *velum,* or *soft palate.*

Most of the time the velum hangs down so that air can flow through your nose for breathing. But when you are speaking, the velum closes off the airflow from the nose so that air flows out of the mouth.

For nasal sounds like *N,* however, the airflow out of the mouth is stopped, and the velum drops to allow the air to flow out of the nose instead.

Therefore the most important difference between the *N* and the non-nasal *L* or *D* sounds is that for *N* the velum is down. The most important difference between *L* and *D* is that *L* is a continuing sound and *D* is a stop, as covered in Unit 9. A practical approach to

teaching students to pronounce these three sounds correctly is to give the class a lot of practice listening to the three different sounds and looking at the pictures of the different tongue positions and airflow patterns. You may want to follow these steps:

1. Ask students to look at the pictures comparing *D* and *N.* Point out that the tongue is actually in the same position, but the difference is in the way the air flows out. No air

flows out of the mouth for either sound, but for *N* it does flow out of the nose. Let students experiment with the words *in, fine,* and *cone* so that they feel the free flow of air through their noses (unless they have colds, in which case the words may sound like *id, fide,* and *code*).

2. Next have students try out contrasting *D* and *N* with pairs of words such as *bed / Ben, Ted / ten* until they can feel the difference between a

---

14 Final sounds N, L, ND, and LD
Linking with N, L, ND, and LD

What's a trail? A path.

A Final sounds N, L, and D

Look at these pictures.

L   N   D

Looking to the side

Air continues out of the mouth | Air continues out of the nose only | Air stops

Looking to the front

bellll | Bennn | bed

Air continues | Air continues | Air stops

B Listening for final sounds N and L

Listen to the final sound of each word. Do not say the words.

1. mine   mile
2. nine   Nile
3. can   call
4. ten   tell
5. man   mall
6. win   will
7. pin   pill
8. when   well

C Which word is different?

1 Listen. Mark the different word.

	X	Y	Z	
1.		✔		(ten, tell, ten)
2.	✓			
3.		✓		
4.			✓	
5.		✓		
6.		✓		
7.			✓	
8.		✓		

2 Listen again.

D Which word do you hear?

1 Listen. Circle the word you hear.

1. (bone)   bowl   (bone)
2. (rain)   rail
3. main   (mail)
4. when   (well)
5. (fine)   file
6. (pain)   pail
7. train   (trail)
8. ten   (tell)

2 Listen again.

don't need to know the meanings of these words. The purpose of the task is just to train their ears to hear the final sound distinction.

C Which word is different?

Have students listen to the audio program and put a checkmark on the different word.

Audio script

1. ten, tell, ten
   /ten/, /tel/, /ten/
2. rain, rail, rail
   /reɪn/, /reɪl/, /reɪl/
3. when, well, when
   /wen/, /wel/, /wen/
4. pin, pin, pill
   /pɪn/, /pɪn/, /pɪl/
5. win, will, win
   /wɪn/, /wɪl/, /wɪn/
6. coal, cone, coal
   /koʊl/, /koʊn/, /koʊl/
7. fine, fine, file
   /faɪn/, /faɪn/, /faɪl/
8. bowl, bone, bowl
   /boʊl/, /boʊn/, /boʊl/

D Which word do you hear?

Have students listen to the audio program and circle the words they hear.

Audio script

1. bone   /boʊn/
2. rain   /reɪn/
3. mail   /meɪl/
4. well   /wel/
5. fine   /faɪn/
6. pain   /peɪn/
7. trail   /treɪl/
8. tell   /tel/

total stoppage of air versus air flowing through the nose.

3. When students understand the difference between *D* and *N*, use the pictures to show how the airflow is different for the *N* and *L* sounds. For the *N* sound the air flows out of the nose; for the *L* sound the air flows out of the mouth. The mirror test in task K on page 105 can also help. (Try this out yourself before you present it to the students.) But *N* and *L* are

also distinguished by their different tongue positions, as students can see in the pictures. Be sure and point this out to your class.

B Listening for final sounds N and L

Have students listen to the audio program and circle the words they hear. Some of these words are defined in exercise H. However, at this point in the course, students

🎧 E Saying final sounds N and L

Have students listen to the audio program and repeat each word they hear at least two times.

Note: The sound *L* can affect the sound of a preceding vowel. That is why the vowels in pairs such as *can* /kæn/ and *call* /kɔːl/ do not sound exactly the same.

🎧 F Saying final sounds ND and LD

Have students listen to the audio program and repeat each word they hear at least two times.

Note: Encourage students to use their ears, not their eyes, to judge the number of syllables in words such as *filed* or *phoned.*

🎧 G Music of English

Have students listen to the audio program and repeat each sentence at least two times.

Note: After students listen to the audio program and repeat the sentences, have them repeat the exchange at least once more as a whole piece, to show how the meanings and intonation patterns of the sentences are linked.

Also remind them that the words *thing* and *stuff* are especially useful for people with limited vocabulary. See K, page T-79 for information on the distinction between *thing* and *stuff.*

🎧 E Saying final sounds N and L

Listen. Say each word two times.

1.	pin	pill	6.	main	mail
2.	win	will	7.	cone	coal
3.	bone	bowl	8.	when	well
4.	rain	rail	9.	then	they'll
5.	can	call	10.	train	trail

🎧 F Saying final sounds ND and LD

Listen. Say each word two times.

1.	find	filed
2.	phoned	fold
3.	trained	trailed
4.	mind	mild
5.	spend	spelled
6.	owned	old

🎧 G Music of English 🎵♪

Listen. Say each sentence two times. Be careful with the final sounds in the most important words.

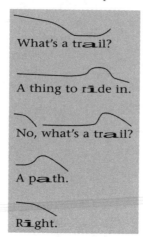

What's a trail?

A thing to ride in.

No, what's a trail?

A path.

Right.

H *Pair work: What's a train for?*

1 Student A, ask question **a** or **b**.

2 Student B, answer.

3 Student A, if the answer is correct, say "Right." If it is wrong, ask again.

4 Take turns asking questions.

Example

> Student A: What's a train for?
> Student B: To walk on.
> Student A: No, what's a **train** for?
> Student B: To ride in.
> Student A: Right.

1. a. What's a trail for?   To walk on.
   b. What's a train for?   To ride in.

2. a. What's a trail?   A path.
   b. What's a train?   A thing to ride in.

3. a. How do you spell "trail"?   T - R - A - I - L.
   b. How do you spell "train"?   T - R - A - I - N.

4. a. What's a pin?   A sharp thing.
   b. What's a pill?   Medicine.

5. a. What's a pin for?   To stick things together.
   b. What's a pill for?   To help a sick person.

6. a. How do you spell "main"?   M - A - I - N.
   b. How do you spell "mail"?   M - A - I - L.

7. a. How do you spell "fold"?   F - O - L - D.
   b. How do you spell "phoned"?   P - H - O - N - E - D.

8. a. What does "fold" mean?   To put one part on top of another part.
   b. What does "phoned" mean?   The past of "phone."

9. a. How do you spell "owned"?   O - W - N - E - D.
   b. How do you spell "old"?   O - L - D.

Unit 14 • **103**

tense *-ed* ending are presented in Unit 5, page 33.

💡 *Teaching Tip*

This task gives students the opportunity to practice pronouncing the final sounds *N, L, ND,* and *LD.* For further practice in pronouncing final *N,* students can suggest a list of objects on the board (e.g., *computers, cars, bicycles,* etc.) and then ask three or four other students *Do you own a ____?* At the end, tally the number of persons owning these objects.

H *Pair work: What's a train for?*

Go over the instructions, modeling the examples with someone in the class. Then put students into pairs and have them do the pair work. Remind them to choose questions **a** or **b** at random to keep the task challenging.

Note: Less familiar words such as *fold* are included to encourage students to practice asking the meaning or spelling of a new word, and also to notice the final consonant or consonant cluster (e.g., *-ld*). In this case you can also point out that because *fold* ends in *-d,* it will gain an extra syllable for the *-ed* ending in the past tense. On the other hand, the verbs *phone* and *own,* used in this task, do not end in either *-d* or *-t,* so they do not have an extra syllable for the *-ed* ending. These rules concerning the past

🎧 I Linking with L, N, LD, and ND

Have students listen to the audio program and repeat the words and sentences they hear at least two times.

You could ask students to find the four instances of final silent -e in the blue boxes before they listen: *phone, called, are, spelled*.

Note: The sound *L* in *call* is a continuing sound, so the linking can be made by drawing out the sound in an exaggerated link. But *D* is a stop sound, so *Hold on* and *Spend it* run together abruptly, causing the last words to sound like "don" and "dit."

🎧 J Pair work: Checking information

Have students listen to the audio program and then say the conversations at least two times. The second time they say the conversations, they should switch roles.

These dialogues are meant to reinforce the use of intonational emphasis to confirm information or correct misunderstandings. This is the way English speakers help the listener to follow. Without this crucial signal, the listener might miss the speaker's meaning, causing a breakdown in communication.

🔆 Teaching Tip

These dialogues could be acted as brief skits, if the students are advanced enough so that they can memorize the lines and then concentrate on how to say them.

🎧 I Linking with L, N, LD, and ND

1 Listen. Say these words two times.

Call our friends.	Callllour friends.
Hold on.	Holdon .
Spend it.	Spendit .
phone number	phonennnumber

2 Listen. Say each sentence two times.

1. We call our friends. We callllour friends.
2. We called our boss. We calledour boss.
3. Hold on tight. Holdon tight.
4. They can always go. They cannnalways go.
5. When are you coming? Whennnare you coming?
6. Don't spend all the money. Don't spendall the money.
7. She spelled every word right. She spelledevery word right.
8. What's your phone number? What's your phonennnumber ?

🎧 J Pair work: Checking information

1 Listen to the conversations.

2 Say the conversations with a partner.

1. The Emergency
   Aunt: The baby swallowed a pill!
   Mother: A pin! Call the doctor!
   Aunt: Not a **pin**, a **pill**.
   Mother: Pin or pill, we have to call the doctor!

2. In a Downtown Office Building
   Visitor: Excuse me, where's the main office?
   Clerk: The main office? Do you mean where you can get information?
   Visitor: No, I mean where I can buy stamps.
   Clerk: Oh, you mean "**mail**"!
   Visitor: Yes, the mail office.
   Clerk: Actually, it's called the **post** office. It's in the next building to the right, and there's a mailbox in front of it.

3. The Misunderstanding

Father: Did you fold them?
Son: Fold what?
Father: The shirts I left for you to fold.
Son: Did you say "**fold them**"? I thought you said "**Phone Tim**."
Father: Did you phone Tim?
Son: Yes! I told him you left some shirts. He thought it was strange!

K   *The mirror test: Final sounds N and L*   EXTRA

1 Find a small mirror and follow these steps.

1. Hold the mirror close to your face, under your nose.
2. Say the sound N strongly.
3. Quickly look at the mirror. You should see a cloud.

Nnnnn

4. Say the word "bone." You should see a cloud again.
5. Say the sound L strongly. You should not see a cloud.

Lllll

6. Say the word "bowl." You should not see a cloud.

2 Try the mirror test with the words below. Check your mirror after each word.

cone   coal
seen   seal
ten   tell
can   call
pin   pill

Unit 14 • **105**

two clouds, but some just make one cloud.

To help students see the cloud more clearly, you could ask them to make the *N* with force, "like a dragon breathing fire."

Another way to use a mirror is to ask students to watch with the mirror in front of their mouths as they say the sounds. When they say *L*, they should be able to see a space on either side of the tongue tip for air to come out. When they say *N*, they should not be able to see any space for air to come out (it can only come out of the nose).

Yet another way to sense the difference between the two sounds is to gently hold the bridge of the nose (near the base of the bony part) with thumb and forefinger, without squeezing. The nose should vibrate when saying *N*, and not vibrate when saying *L*.

Try these techniques yourself before presenting them to the class.

See Unit 14 Quiz on page T-144.

K   *The mirror test: Final sounds N and L*   EXTRA

This task is meant to help students who are having difficulty producing word-final *N*s and *L*s correctly.

To do this activity, you will need to have several small mirrors. A compact cosmetic mirror will work fine, and students may actually have these with them. It is also possible to use polished steel (like a Boy Scout mirror).

A cold mirror works best to condense the moisture from the air flow, so this test may not work well on a hot day. Also, it is easier to see the "cloud" distinction in individual sounds than to see it in words. A word that ends in *L* may have some slight clouding of the mirror, but a word that ends in *N* will have much more clouding.

Students may find the following anatomical fact interesting: Some noses make

15 *Final sounds S, TH, and T*
Linking with TH

Unit overview

In this unit, students will practice distinguishing between and pronouncing the final sounds *S*, *TH*, and *T* (/s/, /θ/, and /t/). They will also practice linking with *TH*, continue to practice the skills of checking and correcting information, and review all the categories of linking they have learned in this course.

🎧 **A** *Final sounds S, TH, and T*

When attempting to say the English *TH* sound, which is a relatively rare sound in the world's languages, some students tend to substitute /t/ and others substitute /s/, depending on the phonology of their first language.

1. Call students' attention to the mouth illustrations. Point out the blue area that shows the shape of the mouth opening (there is no opening for *T*). Give them lots of time to experiment with making these sounds while looking at the pictures. The better they can understand what their mouths are doing, the more clearly they will be able to make the sounds. Then play the audio program.

Note: TH is not really a crucial sound for beginners, because it is not used to convey a grammatical signal. However, it is included here because so many students are puzzled by it, and because it makes such a good contrastive image when compared with other sounds.

---

15 *Final sounds S, TH, and T*
Linking with TH

What's a bath for? To get clean.

🎧 **A** Final sounds S, TH, and T

1 Look at these pictures.

S   TH   T

Looking to the front

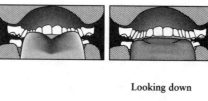

Looking down

mass   math   mat

Air continues   Air continues   Air stops

In the *Looking to the front* pictures, students can see clearly how different the flat tongue shape is for *TH*, in contrast to the V-shaped channel for *S* and the complete blockage for *T*.

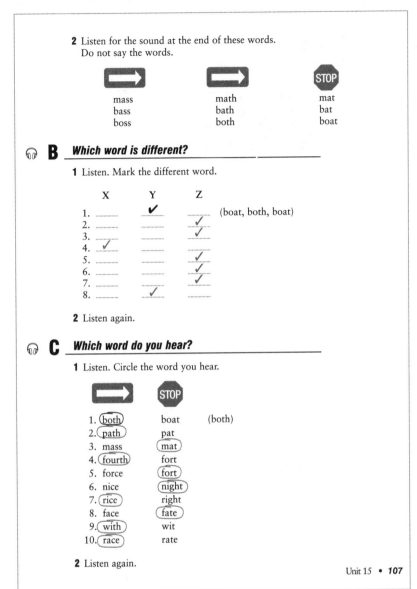

2 Listen for the sound at the end of these words.
Do not say the words.

⟶	⟶	STOP
mass	math	mat
bass	bath	bat
boss	both	boat

🎧 **B** **Which word is different?**

1 Listen. Mark the different word.

	X	Y	Z	
1.		✔		(boat, both, boat)
2.			✓	
3.			✓	
4.	✓			
5.			✓	
6.			✓	
7.			✓	
8.		✓		

2 Listen again.

🎧 **C** **Which word do you hear?**

1 Listen. Circle the word you hear.

⟶	STOP	
1. (both)	boat	(both)
2. (path)	pat	
3. mass	(mat)	
4. (fourth)	fort	
5. force	(fort)	
6. nice	(night)	
7. (rice)	right	
8. face	(fate)	
9. (with)	wit	
10. (race)	rate	

2 Listen again.

Unit 15 • **107**

Audio script

1. boat, both, boat
   /boʊt/, /boʊθ/, /boʊt/
2. bath, bath, bat
   /bæθ/, /bæθ/, /bæt/
3. mass, mass, math
   /mæs/, /mæs/, /mæθ/
4. nice, night, night
   /naɪs/, /naɪt/, /naɪt/
5. rate, rate, race
   /reɪt/, /reɪt/, /reɪs/
6. rice, rice, right
   /raɪs/, /raɪs/, /raɪt/
7. mouth, mouth, mouse
   /maʊθ/, /maʊθ/, /maʊs/
8. fourth, fort, fourth
   /fɔːrθ/, /fɔːrt/, /fɔːrθ/

🎧 **C** **Which word do you hear?**

Have students listen to the audio program and circle the words they hear.

Alternatively, to give students a chance to work in a more active mode, have them respond to each word by holding up a hand for *stop* or drawing a line in the air for *continue*.

Audio script

1. both	/boʊθ/
2. path	/pæθ/
3. mat	/mæt/
4. fourth	/fɔːrθ/
5. fort	/fɔːrt/
6. night	/naɪt/
7. rice	/raɪs/
8. fate	/feɪt/
9. with	/wɪθ/
10. race	/reɪs/

2. Point out to students the vowel sound difference in *boss* /bɔːs/ vs. *both* and *boat* (/boʊθ/ and /boʊt/).

🎧 **B** **Which word is different?**

In this task, students practice listening for the difference between final *S*, *TH*, and *T*. The final sounds *S* and *TH* can be difficult to distinguish, especially on an audio program, even for native speakers. It can be helpful to read the audio script to the class.

T-107

 D Saying final TH

As students look again at the illustration of a mouth saying *TH*, point out how flat the tongue is as the air flows over it. Then play the audio program and have students repeat each word at least two times.

This is the first time that students are being asked to say the *TH* sound aloud, and some of them may feel awkward or self-conscious about it. You can help them relax by being a bit silly yourself. Model the pronunciation of these words, but exaggerate the final *TH*; make it extra loud and long.

Note: It is better not to ask students to stick their tongues out between their teeth. This is disturbing for many people and is not necessary to make the sound clearly.

☆ Teaching Tip

Here is another way to help students distinguish the pronunciation of the *S* and *TH* sounds. Have them say the sounds and hold each one for several seconds. As they say the sounds, they should hold their hands or a piece of tissue about an inch away from their mouths. When they say *TH*, they will feel their breath on their fingers, or the tissue will flutter. When they say *S*, they will feel almost no breath on their fingers, or the tissue will stay nearly still.

D E Saying final TH and T/D in numbers

Play the audio program and have students repeat each number at least two times.

D Saying final TH

1 Look again at the picture of how to say **TH**.

2 Listen. Say each word two times.

1. bath
2. both
3. teeth
4. math
5. mouth

E Saying final TH and T/D in numbers

Listen. Say each number two times.

1. first	first
2. second	second
3. third	third
4. fourth	fourth*th*
5. fifth	fifth*thth*
6. sixth	sixth*thth*
7. seventh	seventh*thth*
8. eighth	eighth*thth*
9. ninth	ninth*thth*
10. tenth	tenth*thth*

☆ Teaching Tip

Go around the room and have each student state his or her birthday using ordinal numbers. The other students should write down the birthdays they hear. Make a note of the birthdays as students say them, and when they are all finished, write the birthdays on the board so students can check what they wrote.

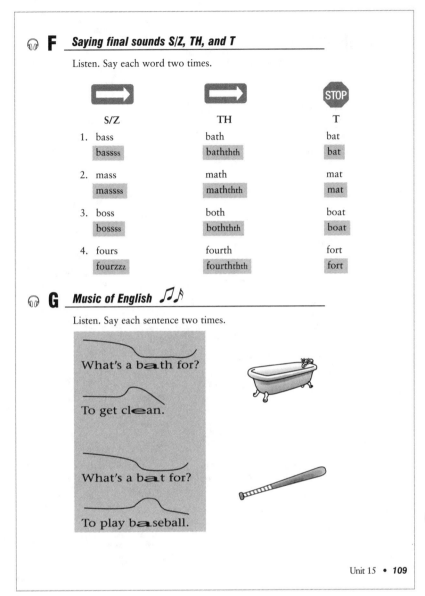

Words with final *S/Z*:

base	please	has
rice	is	dress
close	us	use

A^y _____   A _____
I^y _____   I _____
E^y _____   E _____
O^w _____   O _____
U^w _____   U _____

Ask students to look at the words and write them in the correct columns. Then ask students to say the words. Repeat the procedure with final *TH* and *T*.

Words with final *TH*:

bath	faith	teeth
with	both	Seth
truth		

Words with final *T*:

cute	bat	bait
it	but	not
beat	bed	boat
write		

Note: There are no common words for some combinations of vowel sounds + final sounds.

🎧 G Music of English

Have students listen to the audio program and repeat each sentence at least two times.

A *bat* is also used for cricket. Use whichever game is better known by your students.

Note: After students listen to the audio program and repeat the sentences, have them repeat the exchange at least once more as a whole piece, to show how the meanings and intonation patterns of the sentences are linked.

🎧 F Saying final sounds S/Z, TH, and T

Have students listen to the audio program and repeat each word at least two times.

💡 Teaching Tip

Another way to practice the final sounds *S/Z*, *TH*, and *T* is to focus on the vowel sounds in words that end with these sounds. When students' attention is diverted to another element, it makes the practice more difficult and more like the demands of an actual conversation in which the subject matter distracts from attention to pronunciation.

Review the One Vowel Rule and Two Vowel Rule on pages 19 and 20. Write words with final *S/Z* on the board, and set up two columns of answer blanks beneath them, one for alphabet vowel sounds and one for relative vowel sounds.

H Pair work: What's a bath for?

This task is a review of useful sentences students have learned so far in this course. Since the word order of the auxiliary *do* is particularly difficult for students to master, repeated practice of this sort of construction is important.

💡 Teaching Tip

Play Bingo to help students practice the distinction between *S*, *TH*, and *T*. Here's how:

1. Make Bingo cards with grids of four columns across and four rows down on each card. Each card should have 16 empty boxes or cells. Fill the boxes with words from the list below. Use different words or put them in a different order on each card.

bass	mass	boss
bath	math	both
bat	mat	boat
fours	fourth	fort
rice	path	face
right	pat	fate
race	mouse	faith
rat	mouth	

2. Direct students to mark the word they hear.

3. Have a student (the caller) call out the words from the list in random order (or read them yourself).

4. The first student to get four words in a row (across or down) should call out *Bingo!* loud enough for everyone to hear.

5. Check with the class to see if that student is correct, that is, if all four words have actually been called out. If they have, that student is the next caller, calling out words in random order.

H Pair work: What's a bath for?

1 Student A, ask question **a** or **b**.

2 Student B, answer.

3 Student A, if the answer is correct, say "Right." If it is wrong, ask again.

4 Take turns asking questions.

Examples

> Student A: How do you spell "bat"?
> Student B: B - A - T - H.
> Student A: No. How do you spell "bat"?
>
> Student B: What's a bath for?
> Student A: To get clean.
> Student B: Right.

1. a. How do you spell "bath"?   B - A - T - H.
   b. How do you spell "bat"?   B - A - T.

2. a. What's a bath for?   To get clean.
   b. What's a bat for?   To play baseball.

3. a. What does "both" mean?   Two things. Not just one of them.
   b. What does "boat" mean?   A small ship.

4. a. What does "bath" mean?   A tub, in the bathroom.
   b. What does "bass" mean?   A kind of fish.

5. a. How do you spell "faith"?   F - A - I - T - H.
   b. How do you spell "face"?   F - A - C - E.

6. a. What does "math" mean?   Work with numbers.
   b. What does "mat" mean?   A small rug.

7. a. How do you spell "math"?   M - A - T - H.
   b. How do you spell "mass"?   M - A - S - S.

8. a. What does "mouse" mean?   A small animal.
   b. What does "mouth" mean?   It's used for eating and speaking.

9. a. What comes after "night"? Day.
   b. What comes after "ninth"? Tenth.

10. a. What's a path? A small trail.
    b. What's a pass? A free ticket.

I Pair work: Checking days and dates

1 Student A, say a day, month, and date from the box.

2 Student B, check what your partner said.

3 Student A, if the answer is correct, say "Right."
   If it is wrong, give the correct answer.

4 Take turns saying the days and dates.

Examples

Student A: Tuesday, March first.
Student B: Did you say "Thursday"?
Student A: No, **"Tuesday."**

Student B: Monday, April fourth.
Student A: Did you say "April fifth"?
Student B: No, "April **fourth**."

Day	Month	Date
Monday	January	first
Tuesday	February	second
Wednesday	March	third
Thursday	April	fourth
Friday	May	fifth
Saturday	June	sixth
Sunday	July	seventh
	August	eighth
	September	ninth
	October	tenth
	November	
	December	

Unit 15 • *111*

Teaching Tip

Make two different versions of a calendar for next month, entering different school events, birthdays, or holidays on each one. Put students into pairs. Student A gets a copy of one calendar and Student B gets the other. They should then ask each other for information as they did in the map exercise on pages 88–90. For a more challenging activity, distribute copies of a newspaper page with a calendar of events, and have students fill in separate (blank) calendars with three or four events to ask/tell each other about.

I Pair work: Checking days and dates

Go over the instructions, modeling the examples with someone in the class. Then put students into pairs and have them do the pair work. Remind them to choose from the different columns at random to keep the task interesting.

Note: When *TH* is the final sound in the answers with dates, it should be said clearly. If another word follows (except one beginning with a vowel), the *TH* will probably be dropped. However, when verifying or confirming information, the sounds of the crucial word must be said with extra care, including the *TH* sound. Sentence emphasis is always more important than any other factor in the sentence.

J Linking with TH

Have students listen to the audio program and repeat the phrases and sentences they hear at least two times. This task may be especially useful for learners who have trouble pronouncing *TH* in the final position.

K Review: Linking

This task reviews linking many different sounds, with more than one link in each sentence.

Have students listen to the audio program and repeat each sentence at least two times. Items **7**, **8**, **9**, **10** all practice *TH* linked to *TH*. Note that the sound is not said two times, but simply takes longer to say. Whenever the same sound links two words, it is said as the same sound, only longer.

J Linking with TH

1 Listen to these groups of words.

both of them → boththof them
Fourth of July → Fourththof July
math and English → maththand English
both things → boththththings

2 Listen. Say each sentence two times.

1. I want a bath after dinner. → I want a baththafter dinner.
2. It was the Fourth of July. → It was the Fourththof July.
3. Both of them came. → Boththof them came.
4. Sue is studying math and English. → Sue is studying maththand English.
5. Her teeth are very white. → Her teethththare very white.
6. The path over the mountain is hard. → The paththover the mountain is hard.
7. The path through the woods is easy. → The paththththrough the woods is easy.
8. We both think you should come. → We boththththink you should come.
9. They both thank you. → They boththththank you.
10. He left both things at home. → He left boththththings at home.

K Review: Linking

Listen. Say each sentence two times.

1. Continuing sound + vowel sound

When is the store open? → Whennnis the storerropen?
Will it open before eight? → Willlit open beforerreight?

2. Stop sound + vowel sound

The bank opens at eight.   The bankopens ateight .

I'd like a cup of tea.   I'd likea cupof tea.

3. Continuing sound + continuing sound

She wants fish.   She wantsssfish .

The store's near Main.   The storezzznearrrMain .

4. Vowel sound + vowel sound.

Does he ever drink coffee or tea?   Does heeeever drink coffeeeor tea?

Make the dog go away.   Make the dog goooaway .

She adores vanilla ice cream.   Sheeeadores vanillaaaice cream.

5. Same sound + same sound

Will Lucy arrive soon?   WillllLucy arrive soon?

Please stop pushing!   Pleasezzstoppushing !

6. Linking a group of words

Go away! Far away!   Goooaway! Farrraway !

Come again whenever you want to.   Comemmagain wheneverrryou wantto .

Will it open at ten?   Willllitopennnattnten ?

Will it open before nine?   Willllitopen beforerrnine ?

Bob ate all of the fish soup.   Bobatealllof the fishshshsoup .

 Teaching Tips

If this task is too hard to say smoothly because there are so many syllables and links, use the backward buildup technique described in task H on page T-15.

The sentences in this linking task can also be used to review syllable number. Ask students to count the numbers of syllables in each sentence. They should then compare their answers with a partner. Since missing (or added) syllables are such a common error, it is helpful to focus attention on this subject whenever there is time left in a lesson.

Organize students into small teams. Give each team a short paragraph from a magazine or newspaper and tell them to look for five good spots for linking words. Have them practice these links and then perform them for another team.

Each team should then experiment with the other teams' set of links.

See Unit 15 Quiz on page T-145.

16 Review

Unit overview

This unit gives students a chance to review and consolidate everything they have learned in this course. It also includes a series of *Check yourself* tasks so students can find out how much they have accomplished and what areas they still need to work on. The dialogues and *Music of English* tasks are a bit more extended than those in earlier units, so students should be able to sense how much they have progressed.

A Counting syllables: The Sunshine Cafe

Have students look at the menu for the Sunshine Cafe. Tell them to read the menu while they listen to the audio program, and then to answer the questions in step 2. This menu will be used for subsequent tasks that will serve to review all the various elements of spoken language that have been taught in this course.

Teaching Tip

To start a discussion about what students like in sandwiches, ask them to count which ingredients (foods) they have actually eaten. They may have eaten some of these ingredients without knowing what they are called. If students are not sure what some of these foods are, ask other students to explain, but if they cannot, below are some "definitions" to help them. Using these food names in discussion (Did they like it?) can help them

learn the vocabulary and pronunciation before they fill in the chart on page 115.
Sandwich Ingredients
1. *Hot peppers* do not have a high temperature, but they have a hot flavor. *Bell peppers* are sweet, not hot.
2. *Barbecued beef* is cooked with a sauce made of tomato and brown sugar. *Corned beef* is preserved with salt and spices.
3. *Baked chicken* is baked in an

oven. *Smoked chicken* is cooked slowly over a wood fire. (Students may be more familiar with *fried chicken*, which is deep-fat fried. It is common in fast-food restaurants but not usually an ingredient of sandwiches.)
4. *Pickles* are cucumbers that have been placed in salt water or vinegar for a long time. *Mayonnaise* is a white, creamy sauce used on sandwich bread or in salads.

---

16 Review

A Counting syllables: The Sunshine Cafe ☐ ☐ ☐

1 Listen to the menu for the Sunshine Cafe.

2 Write the answers to these questions.

1. Write the name of one of the sandwiches. ....
2. How many syllables are in the name of this sandwich? ....
3. How many syllables are in the first food in the sandwich? ....
4. Which beverage has the most syllables? ....
5. How many syllables does it have? ....

3 Listen to the menu again. Check your answers.

114 • Unit 16

B Sounds and syllables chart

Write one word from the menu in each box in the chart.
You can use the same word in two boxes.

	One syllable	Two syllables	Three syllables
Two Vowel Rule Circle the alphabet vowel.	b(a)ked m(i)le wh(i)te sm(o)ked wh(o)le cr(e)am wh(ea)t b(ee)f (i)ced ch(ee)se C(o)ke pl(ai)n t(ea)	r(o)asted p(ea)nut c(o)ffee	artich(o)ke tomat(o)es p(i)neapple mayonn(ai)se barbec(ue)d lemon(a)de
One Vowel Rule Circle the relative vowel.	f(i)sh (a)nd Fr(e)nch r(e)d m(i)lk b(e)ll h(o)t (e)gg	p(e)ppers l(e)ttuce j(e)lly ch(i)cken pean(u)t p(i)ckles sal(a)d m(u)stard c(o)ffee b(u)tter	l(e)monade s(a)ndw(i)ches art(i)choke pine(a)pple cuc(u)mbers
Strong syllables Circle the strong syllable.	*(shaded)*	(pe)ppers (le)ttuce (sa)lad (chick)en (co)ffee (pick)les (je)lly (mu)stard (on)ions (bu)tter (sun)-dried (spark)ling (wa)ter (roas)ted (pea)nut	(sand)wiches (ar)tichoke to(ma)toes (bar)becued lemo(nade) (pine)apple cu(cum)bers (may)onnaise
Final stop sounds Circle the final stop sound.	h o(t) mos(t) corne(d) bake(d) eg(g) re(d) whea(t) smoke(d) whi(te) brea(d) an(d) ice(d) mil(k) Co(ke)	mustar(d) roaste(d) sun-drie(d) peanu(t) sala(d) sparklin(g)	articho(ke) barbecue(d) lemona(de)
Final continuing sounds Circle the final continuing sound.	bel(l) fi(sh) choi(ce) crea(m) t(ea) chee(se) rol(l) bee(f) who(le) plai(n) mi(le)	chicke(n) lettu(ce) jell(y) onion(s) tun(a) pepper(s) coffe(e) pickle(s) wate(r) butte(r)	mayonnai(s)e sandwiche(s) tomatoe(s) pineapp(le) cucumber(s)

Unit 16 • **115**

B Sounds and syllables chart

This task gives students a sense of how much they have learned during the course. The chart tests their grasp of some of the basic concepts covered in Units 1–15: alphabet vowels and relative vowels, syllable number and strength, and the distinction between stops and continuing sounds.

Have students write at least two words from the menu in each box in the chart. Tell them that there are many possible answers for each box, and that they can use the same word more than once. They can work individually, in pairs, or in groups. As they are working, copy the chart (without the examples and instructions) onto the board. Either have students go to the board and fill in the boxes, or elicit answers from the whole class when they are finished.

💡 Teaching Tip

You can do this task as a group race. Put students in small groups and have them fill in the chart as quickly as they can. After a reasonable amount of time, tell students to stop working and check answers as a class. The group that had the largest number of correct answers wins.

C *Music of English*

On the audio program, students will hear the conversation as a whole piece, rather than broken up into lines. Have them listen and then practice the whole conversation with a partner at least two times. They should switch roles the second time they practice.

It is natural for students to lapse back into the rhythm of their first language when they have been focusing on other aspects of language, or thinking about meaning. Be aware of this tendency, and, if it occurs, remind them about lengthening the vowel in the strong syllable of the most important word. It can be very helpful to occasionally refresh their awareness of rhythm by using choral repetition of a sentence. In choral recitation, students reinforce each others' sense of rhythm, as they tend to fall into rhythmic harmony with the group voice. This strengthens their sense of the variable length of syllables, which is so characteristic of English.

Teaching Tip

Since many repetitions increase the exact rhythmic control, vary the repetition drill by asking them to do it with whispering, instead of speaking. Whispering concentrates the mind because it is such a change, and rhythm can be heard quite well without the voice.

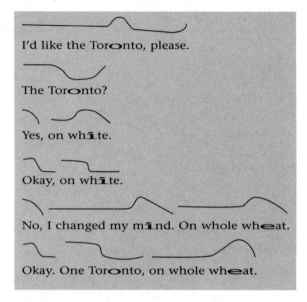

C Music of English

Listen. Say the conversation two times.

I'd like the Toronto, please.

The Toronto?

Yes, on white.

Okay, on white.

No, I changed my mind. On whole wheat.

Okay. One Toronto, on whole wheat.

D Pair work: The most important word

1 Listen to these conversations. Circle the most important word in each sentence.

2 Say the conversations with a partner. Take turns as the customer and the server.

1. Customer: I'd like the Toronto, please.
   Server: The Toronto?
   Customer: Yes, on whole wheat.
   Server: Okay. One Toronto, on whole wheat. Coming right up!

D *Pair work: The most important word*

Play the audio program for students, then have them circle what they think is the most important word in each sentence.

Answers may vary slightly. Tell students that this is not a problem, as people's ideas of what word is most important can differ.

2. Customer: I'd like the (Honolulu), please.
    Server: Okay, (one) Honolulu. What kind of (bread)?
Customer: Whole (wheat). No, I changed my (mind).
    I'd like the (San Francisco).
    Server: (One) San Francisco. On a (French roll)?
Customer: That sounds (good).
    Server: And to (drink)?
Customer: (Tea).
    Server: (Hot) tea?
Customer: No, (iced) tea.
    Server: (Thank) you.

E | *Pair work: Finding the most important word*

1 Read these conversations. Discuss with your partner which words are most important. Circle the most important words.

2 Take turns as the customer and the server.

1. The Happy Customer

    Customer: What's the (best) sandwich?
        Server: The (Honolulu).
    Customer: Is that the one with
        (pineapple)?
        Server: Yes. And (chicken).
    Customer: (Smoked) chicken?
        Server: No, (baked) chicken.
    Customer: That sounds (fine)!

Specials

2. The Difficult Server

    Customer: I'd like the (San Francisco), please.
        Server: No (fish) today.
    Customer: Well, then I'd like the (Toronto).
        Server: No (chicken) today.
    Customer: Do you have (anything)?
        Server: (Cheese). But the cheese is (bad).
    Customer: Then just bring me (coffee).

E | *Pair work: Finding the most important word*

Have students read the conversations, and then, with a partner, circle the words they think are most important. Remind them that it is not a problem if their answers are slightly different, but that when one speaker is correcting something the other speaker said, the corrected word is always stressed.

 *Teaching Tip*

An excellent way for students to check their ability to make clear which words are important is to have Student A circle the most important words in a dialogue and then read it aloud to Student B, without showing Student B which words were marked. Student B should mark the words he or she thinks were emphasized, and show the results to Student A. This kind of checking works best with a short dialogue (or paragraph) that the partners have not previously practiced. The listener's focus should be not on what words he or she would emphasize, but to listen for the word the speaker actually *did* emphasize. If the listener is uncertain, a question mark can be placed next to the sentence.

It can work very well to have one student read aloud to a whole class and have them all mark the emphasis they think they heard. Because emphasis ("topic focus") is marked in different ways by different languages, students need as much practice as possible doing it according to the specifically English system.

🎧 **F** *Music of English*

Again, students will hear the conversation as a whole piece, rather than broken up into sentences. After they listen, have them repeat the conversation at least two times. They should switch roles the second time they practice.

Have students practice this conversation with several partners. Because everybody – even speakers with the same first language – has a somewhat different way of speaking, it is important for students to learn to tolerate variations in what they hear. If learners hear exactly the same model each time (in a recording, for instance), they will not be so able to adjust to the actual conditions of real conversation in the new language.

Note: Some students may be uncomfortable using the word *hate*, but most will enjoy being able to express some strong feeling. If they are enjoying it, you could give them some further expressions such as *I think barbecued beef is **aw**ful!* or *Barbecued beef is **terr**ible!* If they want a milder way to say this, suggest *I don't **like** barbecued beef,* or *I don't **care** for barbecued beef.*

---

3. The Difficult Customer

Customer: Bring me a Toronto.
   Server: That's with chicken.
Customer: No, I want beef.
   Server: The Dallas has beef.
Customer: Barbecued beef?
   Server: Yes.
Customer: Oh, no! I hate barbecued beef! I'll have the one with fish.
   Server: Okay, one San Francisco. And to drink?
Customer: Coffee. But it has to be hot. Really hot.
   Server: Okay. Whatever will make you happy.

🎧 **F** *Music of English* ♫♪

Listen. Say this conversation two times.

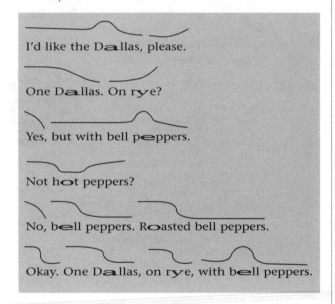

I'd like the Dallas, please.

One Dallas. On rye?

Yes, but with bell peppers.

Not hot peppers?

No, bell peppers. Roasted bell peppers.

Okay. One Dallas, on rye, with bell peppers.

G *Pair work: Ordering at the Sunshine Cafe*

1 Work with a partner. Take turns as the customer and the server.

2 Customer, order a sandwich from the menu on page 114.

3 Server, check to make sure you understood.

4 Customer, say Yes, correct an error, or change your mind.

H *Check yourself: Syllables, linking, and most important words*

1 Record yourself saying the conversation. Say both parts, **X** and **Y**. (If you do not have a tape recorder, ask a partner to listen.)

The Beach

Line
1 X: We rented a car.
2 Y: You painted a car?
3 X: No, we rented a car.
4   We went to the beach.
5 Y: When did you go?
6 X: Wednesday.
7 Y: But it was raining!
8 X: That's okay. When we
9   plan a trip, we go!

2 Listen to your tape three times. Each time, complete a checklist below. (If you are working with a partner, say the conversation three times, one for each checklist. Your partner can complete the checklists.)

Checklist 1: Syllables
Did you get the right number of syllables in these words?

Line		Yes	No	
1	rented			(2)
2	painted			(2)
6	Wednesday			(2)
7	raining			(2)
9	plan			(1)

G *Pair work: Ordering at the Sunshine Cafe*

Go over the instructions with students, then model the task with someone in the class. Tell students they can use the *Music of English* conversation in F to help them. Then put them into pairs and have them complete the pair work.

 **Teaching Tip**

If you have access to some authentic English-language menus and you feel that your class is ready for the challenge, make enough copies of the menus for each pair of students. Have them use the authentic menus to do the pair work.

Encourage students to be dramatic or humorous when doing this pair work (the final one in the course). For example, they may want to make the customer very demanding, asking for things that are not on the menu, or they may want to make the server very stubborn. If time allows, let students write their conversations as skits, practice them, and perform them for the whole class. This could be an enjoyable final class activity.

H *Check yourself: Syllables, linking, and most important words*

For the three tasks (H, I, and J on pages 119 through 123), the procedure is the same.

It is best if each pair of students can use a tape recorder and record the dialogue on an audio cassette. Then they listen to the recording three times, each time completing a different checklist. You could assign this as out-of-class work if it proves impossible to have enough tape recorders for all pairs of students. In addition, it is best for students to record their conversations in places without much background noise.

If no tape recorders are available, students can work in groups of three. Two students will say the conversation three times while a third student listens and completes the checklists. If you use this method, be sure that listening students have the chance to do the speaking part of the task as well.

I Check yourself: Final sounds, linking, and most important words

Follow the procedure in H, page T-119.

💡 Teaching Tip

If there is time for follow-up work, videotape a short segment from a television drama and prepare a script of the segment for students to read. A soap opera is best because it usually has slow-paced, but natural, language and is likely to be dramatic. Then follow these steps:

1. Play the segment several times without sound and ask students to notice the "body language." They should focus on emphasis, which may just be shown in the face, but may involve more of the body in dramatic scenes.

2. Play the segment with the sound on.

3. Play it again and have students read the script of the scene and circle the most important words.

4. Have students practice each line in a choral fashion, perhaps stepping around the room, emphasizing the most important words with a long, swooping step on the strong syllable.

5. If students can say the sentences with confidence, put them into small groups to practice playing the scene.

6. Now they can perform the scene for the class.

Checklist 2: Linking
Did you link these words?

Line		Yes	No	
1	rented a	....	....	renteda
2	painted a	....	....	painteda
4	went to	....	....	wentto
7	was raining	....	....	wazzzraining
8	That's okay	....	....	Thatsssokay
9	plan a	....	....	plannna

Checklist 3: Most important words
Did your voice go up or down on these words?

Line		Yes	No	
1	car	....	....	car
2	painted	....	....	painted
3	rented	....	....	rented
4	beach	....	....	beach
5	go	....	....	go
6	Wednesday	....	....	Wednesday
7	raining	....	....	raining
9	plan	....	....	plan
9	go	....	....	go

3 Record the conversation again. (Or, say it again for your partner.) Listen for your improvement.

I Check yourself: Final sounds, linking, and most important words

1 Record yourself saying the conversation. Say both parts, X and Y. (If you do not have a tape recorder, ask a partner to listen.)

A Party

Line
1 X: We're having a party tomorrow night.
2 Y: What kind of party?
3 X: A birthday party.
4 Y: Who's it for?
5 X: My sister. She's going to be nineteen.
6 Y: Who's coming?
7 X: A lot of people.

Line
8   Y: Are all your relatives coming?
9   X: Yes, everybody but Aunt Ann. She's not well.
10 Y: Oh, that's too bad.

2 Listen to your tape three times. Each time, complete a checklist below.
(If you are working with a partner, say the conversation three times,
one for each checklist. Your partner can complete the checklists.)

Checklist 1: Final sounds
Did you say the final sounds clearly in these words?

Line		Yes	No	
1	We're	....	....	➡
2	kind	....	....	STOP
4	Who's	....	....	➡
5	sister	....	....	➡
5	nineteen	....	....	➡
7	lot	....	....	STOP
8	relatives	....	....	➡
9	Aunt	....	....	STOP
10	bad	....	....	STOP

Checklist 2: Linking
Did you link these words?

Line		Yes	No	
2	kind of	....	....	kindof
4	Who's it	....	....	Whozzzit
7	lot of	....	....	lotof
8	Are all	....	....	Arerrall
8	your relatives	....	....	yourrrrelatives
9	She's not	....	....	Shezzznot

J   Review: Syllables, linking, and most important words

Follow the procedure in H, page T-119.

If your students have access to tape recorders, you might find it useful to have them record themselves reading this dialogue, or any one of the dialogues in this unit, early on in the course. If students keep a recording of themselves reading one of these dialogues aloud, they will be able to compare that version with one that they make at the end of the course. They will be astonished at the progress they have made.

Checklist 3: Most important words
Did your voice go up or down on these words?

Line		Yes	No	
1	party	....	....	pa**r**ty
2	kind	....	....	k**i**nd
3	birthday	....	....	b**i**rthday
4	for	....	....	f**o**r
5	sister	....	....	s**i**ster
5	nineteen	....	....	n**i**neteen
6	coming	....	....	c**o**ming
7	lot	....	....	l**o**t
8	relatives	....	....	r**e**latives
9	Ann	....	....	**A**nn
9	well	....	....	w**e**ll
10	bad	....	....	b**a**d

3 Record the conversation again. (Or, say it again for your partner.) Listen for your improvement.

J   Review: Syllables, linking, and most important words

1 Record yourself saying this conversation the same way you did before.

A Trip in the U.S.A.

Line
1   X: I'm planning a trip.
2   Y: A long trip?
3   X: No, just a short one.
4   Y: Where are you going?
5   X: Washington.
6   Y: The capital?
7   X: No, Washington State.
8   Y: That's a long trip!
9   X: Oh, we're flying. So it won't take long.
10 Y: Is this for business?
11 X: No, just for a vacation.
12 Y: Well, have a super trip!

2 Listen to your tape three times. Each time, complete a checklist below.

Checklist 1: Syllables
Did you say the right number of syllables in these words?

Line		Yes	No	
1	planning	....	....	(2)
5	Washington	....	....	(3)
6	capital	....	....	(3)
9	flying	....	....	(2)
10	business	....	....	(2)
11	vacation	....	....	(3)
12	super	....	....	(2)

Checklist 2: Linking
Did you link these words?

Line		Yes	No	
3	just a	....	....	justa
4	Where are you	....	....	Whererrarerryou
8	That's a	....	....	Thatsssa
11	for a	....	....	forrra
12	have a	....	....	havevva

Checklist 3: Most important word
Did your voice go up or down on these words?

Line		Yes	No	
1	trip	....	....	trip
2	long	....	....	long
3	short	....	....	short
4	going	....	....	going
5	Washington	....	....	Washington
6	capital	....	....	capital
7	state	....	....	state
8	long	....	....	long
9	flying	....	....	flying
9	won't	....	....	won't
10	business	....	....	business
11	vacation	....	....	vacation
12	super	....	....	super

3 Now record the conversation again. Listen for how you have improved.

Teaching Tip

As your students finish the course and you say good-bye, leave them with a parting message such as:
"Here is my advice to you. If you are speaking with someone, and they do not understand you, stop a moment and think about the sentence you just said. You do not have time to try to say each sound right. The other person may be in a hurry. The best way to help him or her understand is to decide which word was most important. Then say the sentence again and make sure that you have made the strong syllable in that word very strong. Make the vowel longer. And be sure that you change your voice up or down. This is the best way to make sure you are speaking English clearly.

And if you are not sure what somebody said to you, ask them to repeat it. Listen for the most important word. If it is not clear, ask them about that word. Ask the questions you practiced in the *Music of English*. Ask them, *Did you say ___?* or *What does ____ mean?* Your English is going to get better and better."

Notes on Appendices

Appendix A: Parts of the mouth

This illustration shows an interior side view of the mouth. Students are generally not consciously aware of what is happening inside their mouths, so looking at illustrations of different perspectives can help. The following entertaining procedure can help your students orient themselves to the "geography" of the inside of their mouths. (Before doing it, familiarize yourself with the drawing in Appendix A.) Give students time at each step to become consciously aware of the different parts of the *vocal tract*.

1. NOSE. Draw just a nose on the board, facing to the right, the same way as the picture. Say *nose*.

2. UPPER LIP. Continue the line down from the nose to draw an upper lip, saying, *upper lip*. Ask students to touch the tip of their tongues to their upper lips. (There is no need for them to actually stick their tongues out beyond their upper lips.) Because this is a silent and private activity, even shy students may take part. However, do not insist that students do this; they may simply wish to observe. After this, have students repeat after you the names of the parts introduced so far: *nose, upper lip, tongue, tip*.

3. FRONT TEETH. Continue the line and draw the front teeth (rather V-shaped when looked at from the side). Say *front teeth* and ask students

to follow with the tips of their tongues, down the front of the teeth and up the back of the teeth.

4. TOOTH RIDGE. Now extend the line slightly up and back from the teeth to show the tooth ridge (alveolar ridge). Say *tooth ridge* and ask them to follow this shape with their tongues, up over the bump behind the teeth and up to the roof of the mouth. Many English sounds are made by touching the tongue to the tooth ridge (*N, L, T/D*), and others are made by bringing the tongue near it (*S/Z, SH*).

Appendix B: Tongue shape for T/D, S/Z, L, R, and TH

These photographs and drawings compare the mouth positions for the sounds that are practiced in this book. In field testing, it was found that some students could understand the three-dimensional quality of the mouth better in the photographs, but other students understood better by looking at the drawings. These two kinds of images are placed side-by-side to help students assimilate the information.

When students compare the sounds by looking at the differently shaped openings at the front of the mouth, they can see clearly that the airflow is different for each sound. It is the different configurations of the tongue in the mouth that shape the patterns of sound waves that the listener can hear as different speech sounds. Some of these configurations

are easier to show from the side, and some show more clearly when viewed from the back of the mouth looking to the front. That is why different views are shown in this book.

1. *T/D*. The tongue blocks off air all the way around the tooth ridge (in a horseshoe shape) for *T/D* sounds. *N* is made the same way, but the air flows out through the nose.

2. *S/Z*. The tongue is V-shaped so that air rushes through the narrow constriction and hits the upper front teeth, making the characteristic hissing noise.

3. *L*. The tip of the tongue touches the tooth ridge, keeping the rest of the tongue low so that air can continue to flow out on either side.

4. *R*. The tongue is pulled back so that air can flow over it without any stopping or hissing.

5. *TH*. The tongue is flat so that air can flow out over it without any hissing. One way students can test this is to say the sound in a continuing stream of air and then reverse the flow by drawing air back into the mouth. They should feel cold air flowing over their flat tongues.

It is important to give students enough time to absorb the information they can get from these illustrations and photos. Encourage them to quietly try out the sounds over and over, or allow them to sit and think silently while they look at the pictures. Different students learn differently.

If they have already learned these sounds separately (in preceding units), you can have them review the entire set by asking for choral responses (the whole class) of single words, then moving on to minimal pairs of words, and then to a set for all five sounds. If students repeat words chorally many times, they will gain confidence from each other and will be able to say the sounds more strongly than if they are asked to recite individually.

Sample minimal pairs:

but	bus
made	mail
bet	bear
right	rice
boat	both

Note: Because some people are bothered by photographs of anything inside the body, it might be wise to remind students that the mouths in the photographs are not real, but wax ("plastic") models.

Appendix C: Vowels A^y, I^y, and U^w

Encourage students to notice how the lips and the jaw change position. All the "alphabet vowels" A^y /eɪ/, E^y /iː/, I^y /aɪ/, O^w /ou/, U^w /uː/, have some movement of the tongue and the lips, although some have more than others, making them into actual diphthongs. The tongue moves upward for all five sounds, and this movement upward leads to a change in the position of the lips, with the lips ending in a spread (smiling) position for A^y, E^y, and I^y, or a rounded position for O^w and U^w. The jaw also moves upward, following the tongue.

For the U^w sound, the movement is not large enough to move the jaw much, but the lips end in a very rounded position. Point out how much more the lips stick out for this rounded position than for the spread-lip position. For the O^w sound, because the tongue moves more than for U^w, the jaw also moves visibly. Have students try this jaw and lip rounding movement without making any sound.

Whenever students are asked to look at a drawing, they should be given some time to try out the sounds for themselves.

Appendix D: Vowel rules

The vowel rules are reviewed here, and then lists of new words are given so that students can have the opportunity to practice "sounding out" unfamiliar words. Students may recognize words they have heard but have never read.

Appendix E: How often do the vowel rules work?

These charts show how often the two spelling rules introduced in the book actually work for different vowel letters and letter combinations. Students with a scientific curiosity, or those who doubt the usefulness of learning rules, may appreciate this chart.

Quiz Answer Key

Unit 1 Quiz

A.

	Yes	No	
1.	✓	___	(cake)
2.	___	✓	(Coke)
3.	✓	___	(name)
4.	___	✓	(please)

B.

	Yes	No	
1.	___	✓	(pie)
2.	✓	___	(tea)
3.	✓	___	(cream)
4.	___	✓	(same)

C.

	Yes	No	
1.	✓	___	(fries)
2.	___	✓	(see)
3.	✓	___	(hi)
4.	___	✓	(cream)

D.

	Yes	No	
1.	✓	___	(cone)
2.	✓	___	(slow)
3.	✓	___	(those)
4.	___	✓	(these)

E.

	Yes	No	
1.	✓	___	(cute)
2.	___	✓	(boat)
3.	✓	___	(June)
4.	✓	___	(use)

Unit 2 Quiz

1. name
2. cream
3. pie
4. home
5. seat
6. train
7. same
8. fries
9. fruit
10. read
11. cute
12. rule
13. time
14. use
15. boat
16. these
17. write
18. rain
19. those
20. close

Unit 3 Quiz

1. _1_ (sit)
2. _2_ (raining)
3. _2_ (remain)
4. _3_ (repeated)
5. _3_ (cheeseburger)
6. _1_ (salt)
7. _1_ (please)
8. _2_ (cleaning)
9. _1_ (juice)
10. _2_ (soapy)
11. _2_ (cream pie)
12. _2_ (ice cube)
13. _1_ (milk)
14. _3_ (tomato)
15. _5_ (tomato sandwich)
16. _2_ (excuse)
17. _2_ (arrive)
18. _3_ (seventy)
19. _2_ (city)
20. _5_ (banana milkshake)

Unit 4 Quiz

	X	Y	Z	
1.	___	___	✓	(late, late, let)
2.	___	✓	___	(Jan, Jane, Jan)
3.	___	___	✓	(sit, sit, site)
4.	___	✓	___	(cute, cut, cute)
5.	✓	___	___	(ten, teen, teen)
6.	✓	___	___	(Pete, pet, pet)
7.	___	___	✓	(Jake, Jake, Jack)
8.	___	___	✓	(hope, hope hop)
9.	___	✓	___	(Joan, John, Joan)
10.	___	___	✓	(less, less, lease)

Unit 5 Quiz

1. Chicago
2. washing
3. freezer
4. bathtub
5. creamy
6. telephone
7. computer
8. open
9. newspaper
10. arrive
11. under
12. coffee
13. ceiling
14. cola
15. cleaner
16. using
17. funny
18. market
19. vanilla
20. opener

Unit 6 Quiz

1. pizza
2. chicken
3. lemon
4. sandwich
5. butter
6. vanilla
7. alarm
8. China
9. elephant
10. salad

Unit 7 Quiz

1. What's the matter?
2. I lost my book.
3. Which book?
4. My English book.
5. When did you have it?
6. Yesterday morning.
7. Where were you?
8. On the train.
9. I hope you find it.
10. Me too!

Unit 8 Quiz

	X	Y	Z	
1.	___	___	✓	(had, had, has)
2.	✓	___	___	(rise, ride, ride)
3.	___	___	✓	(road, road, roads)
4.	___	___	✓	(night, night, nice)
5.	___	✓	___	(ticket, tickets, ticket)
6.	✓	___	___	(seats, seat, seat)
7.	___	___	✓	(repeat, repeat, repeats)
8.	___	___	✓	(it, it, is)
9.	___	✓	___	(lemonade, lemonades, lemonade)
10.	___	✓	___	(bus, but, bus)

Unit 9 Quiz

1.	food	(fool)
2.	bed	(bell)
3.	paid	(pail)
4.	(feed)	feel
5.	road	(roll)
6.	wade	(whale)
7.	(tide)	tile
8.	fade	(fail)
9.	made	(mail)
10.	(red)	rail

Unit 10 Quiz

1.	called	(call)
2.	(cold)	coal
3.	(sailed)	sail
4.	(hold)	hole
5.	gold	(goal)
6.	(field)	feel
7.	made	(mail)
8.	filled	(fill)
9.	pulled	(pull)
10.	bold	(bowl)

Unit 11 Quiz

	X	Y	Z	
1.	___	___	✓	(are, are, art)
2.	___	___	✓	(feed, feed, fear)
3.	✓	___	___	(what, where, where)
4.	___	✓	___	(care, cared, care)
5.	___	___	✓	(neat, neat, near)
6.	✓	___	___	(core, code, code)
7.	___	✓	___	(fat, far, fat)
8.	✓	___	___	(paid, pair, pair)
9.	___	✓	___	(tired, tire, tired)
10.	___	✓	___	(roar, roared, roar)

Unit 12 Quiz

	Yes	No	
1.	✓		(parks)
2.	✓		(fries)
3.		✓	(map)
4.		✓	(theater)
5.	✓		(toys)
6.	✓		(parking lots)
7.		✓	(laundromat)
8.	✓		(offices)
9.	✓		(hospitals)
10.		✓	(alley)

Unit 13 Quiz

a.	(30)	13
b.	50	(15)
c.	(60)	16
d.	(90)	19
e.	(80)	18
f.	1980	(1918)
g.	(1990)	1919
h.	(2030)	2013
i.	1950	(1915)
j.	(2060)	2016

Unit 14 Quiz

1.	(mail)	mailed
2.	(when)	well
3.	(train)	trail
4.	ten	(tell)
5.	fill	(filled)
6.	(win)	will
7.	(owned)	old
8.	(phone)	fold
9.	spend	(spelled)
10.	(Bill)	build

Unit 15 Quiz

	X	Y	Z	
1.			✓	(mass, mass, math)
2.		✓		(path, Pat, path)
3.		✓		(bet, Beth, bet)
4.	✓			(nine, ninth, ninth)
5.			✓	(mouth, mouth, mouse)
6.		✓		(boss, both, boss)
7.	✓			(with, wit, wit)
8.		✓		(force, fourth, force)
9.			✓	(tent, tent, tenth)
10.			✓	(faith, faith, face)

Unit Quizzes

Unit 1 Quiz

A. Listen. Do you hear A? Mark Yes or No.

	Yes	No
1.	____	____
2.	____	____
3.	____	____
4.	____	____

B. Listen. Do you hear E? Mark Yes or No.

	Yes	No
1.	____	____
2.	____	____
3.	____	____
4.	____	____

C. Listen. Do you hear I? Mark Yes or No.

	Yes	No
1.	____	____
2.	____	____
3.	____	____
4.	____	____

D. Listen. Do you hear O? Mark Yes or No.

	Yes	No
1.	____	____
2.	____	____
3.	____	____
4.	____	____

E. Listen. Do you hear U? Mark Yes or No.

	Yes	No
1.	____	____
2.	____	____
3.	____	____
4.	____	____

Score _____

10 points total; 1/2 point for each correct answer

Unit 2 Quiz

Listen. Which vowel letter says its alphabet name? Circle the letter.

1. name
2. cream
3. pie
4. home
5. seat
6. train
7. same
8. fries
9. fruit
10. read

11. cute
12. rule
13. time
14. use
15. boat
16. these
17. write
18. rain
19. those
20. close

Score _____

10 points total; 1/2 point for each correct answer

Unit 3 Quiz

Listen. How many syllables are in each word? Write the number.

1. _____   11. _____

2. _____   12. _____

3. _____   13. _____

4. _____   14. _____

5. _____   15. _____

6. _____   16. _____

7. _____   17. _____

8. _____   18. _____

9. _____   19. _____

10. _____   20. _____

Score _____

10 points total; 1/2 point for each correct answer

Name _____ _Date_ _____

Listen to three words. One word is different. Mark it.

	X	Y	Z
1.	___	___	___
2.	___	___	___
3.	___	___	___
4.	___	___	___
5.	___	___	___
6.	___	___	___
7.	___	___	___
8.	___	___	___
9.	___	___	___
10.	___	___	___

Score _____

10 points total; 1 point for each correct answer

Name _____   *Date* _____

Listen for the strong syllable in each word. Circle the long vowel in the strong syllable.

1. Chicago
2. washing
3. freezer
4. bathtub
5. creamy
6. telephone
7. computer
8. open
9. newspaper
10. arrive

11. under
12. coffee
13. ceiling
14. cola
15. cleaner
16. using
17. funny
18. market
19. vanilla
20. opener

Score _____

10 points total; 1/2 point for each correct answer

Name _____ Date _____

Unit 6 Quiz

Listen. Which vowel sounds are weak? Draw a line through the weak vowels.

1. pizza
2. chicken
3. lemon
4. sandwich
5. butter
6. vanilla
7. alarm
8. China
9. elephant
10. salad

Score _____

10 points total; 1 point for each correct answer

Clear Speech from the Start

Unit 7 Quiz

Listen. Circle the most important word in each sentence.

1. What's the matter?
2. I lost my book.
3. Which book?
4. My English book.
5. When did you have it?
6. Yesterday morning.
7. Where were you?
8. On the train.
9. I hope you find it.
10. Me too!

Score _____

10 points total; 1 point for each correct answer

Unit 8 Quiz

Listen. Which word is different? Mark the different word.

	X	Y	Z
1.	___	___	___
2.	___	___	___
3.	___	___	___
4.	___	___	___
5.	___	___	___
6.	___	___	___
7.	___	___	___
8.	___	___	___
9.	___	___	___
10.	___	___	___

Score _____

10 points total; 1 point for each correct answer

T-140 *Clear Speech from the Start*

Unit 9 Quiz

Listen. Which word do you hear? Circle the word.

	STOP	→
1.	food	fool
2.	bed	bell
3.	paid	pail
4.	feed	feel
5.	road	roll
6.	wade	whale
7.	tide	tile
8.	fade	fail
9.	made	mail
10.	red	rail

Score _____

10 points total; 1 point for each correct answer

Unit 10 Quiz

Listen. Which word do you hear? Circle the word.

	STOP	→
1.	called	call
2.	cold	coal
3.	sailed	sail
4.	hold	hole
5.	gold	goal
6.	field	feel
7.	made	mail
8.	filled	fill
9.	pulled	pull
10.	bold	bowl

Score _____

10 points total; 1 point for each correct answer

Unit 11 Quiz

Listen. Which word is different? Mark the different word.

	X	Y	Z
1.	___	___	___
2.	___	___	___
3.	___	___	___
4.	___	___	___
5.	___	___	___
6.	___	___	___
7.	___	___	___
8.	___	___	___
9.	___	___	___
10.	___	___	___

Score _____

10 points total; 1 point for each correct answer

Name _____ Date _____

Listen. Do you hear a final S/Z sound? Mark Yes or No.

	Yes	No
1.	___	___
2.	___	___
3.	___	___
4.	___	___
5.	___	___
6.	___	___
7.	___	___
8.	___	___
9.	___	___
10.	___	___

Score _____

10 points total; 1 point for each correct answer

Unit 13 Quiz

Listen. Which number do you hear? Circle the number.

a.	30	13
b.	50	15
c.	60	16
d.	90	19
e.	80	18
f.	1980	1918
g.	1990	1919
h.	2030	2013
i.	1950	1915
j.	2060	2016

Score _____

10 points total; 1 point for each correct answer

Name _____ Date _____

Unit 14 Quiz

Listen. Which word do you hear? Circle the word.

1.	mail	mailed
2.	when	well
3.	train	trail
4.	ten	tell
5.	fill	filled
6.	win	will
7.	owned	old
8.	phone	fold
9.	spend	spelled
10.	Bill	build

Score _____

10 points total; 1 point for each correct answer

Clear Speech from the Start

Name _____ Date _____

Unit 15 Quiz

Listen. Which word is different? Mark the different word.

	X	Y	Z
1.	____	____	____
2.	____	____	____
3.	____	____	____
4.	____	____	____
5.	____	____	____
6.	____	____	____
7.	____	____	____
8.	____	____	____
9.	____	____	____
10.	____	____	____

Score _____

10 points total; 1 point for each correct answer